Growing Up Southern

by

Betty N. Weaver

Published By
D'AMON PRESS
a division of
VA'APR, INC.

ISBN: 0-914491-24-5

Published By
DAMON PRESS
a division of
VAAPR, INC.
P.O. Box 44370
Baton Rouge, LA 70804

Branch Offices In
New Orleans • Charlotte - Rock Hill • New York City
Fort Worth • San Francisco • San Juan, Puerto Rico

"To Jack, Laura, Becky, and Steve who turned me into a member of the clan."

Chapter 1

Growing Up Southern

Sometimes I think I will write a book, a novel, of course, and tell what it is truly like to be the last of the line and me a girl. I believe I might write about being an only child, an only grandchild, and an only niece growing up in a world where there was much talk of cousins, first, once (and sometimes twice) removed. It was a world of loneliness, love and my growing concern for questioning of values. Yes, sometimes I think I will write that story. It is one I know well.

The best reason for not writing the story is that all the participants aren't dead. They do not remember themselves as I remember them. Since we were all there, we are all selective. Where the truth lies, if there is such a thing, God only knows. I don't pretend to. All I have are memories and traces of where I came from in what I am.

If I ever really considered writing such a book, where would I begin? How could I portray my strange, and sometimes stray, array of relatives with any hope of making them believable, much less letting the reader know how great and truly warm they were?

There was my mother who was strong-willed and, with the instincts of a feminist, living all her life in a Virginia still frozen between centuries. This strong personality cannot be explained in platitudes or endured with consistent patience. How long it took me to learn that I had to deal with her with cold honesty or she would rule me is a story in itself.

I could write about a handsome father with kind blue eyes whom I adored, but could I bring myself to reveal that I learned

1

his secret of dealing with life was to genuflect? I could, perhaps, admit that, if I could also explain that I loved him still.

It will not be easy to write, with any honesty, of a grandfather with an iron will. He always demanded that his world be ordered as he saw it without deviation. There was no "other viewpoint" as far as he was concerned.

I must speak with respect of a grandmother who was the religious backbone of the family. Even now I can close my eyes and see her in her black dress with lace at the throat. Her feet were shod in black lace-up shoes. On her head was a pert black sailor hat. Her long black hair was braided and pinned around her head with bone pins. She wore small pearl earrings in her pierced ears and a gold cross around her neck. She carried a black leather snap purse on her arm and carried her much worn Bible in her other hand. She was going to church. I know now that she was one of those millions of women who give so much of themselves and their time so that such institutions can prosper.

Some of my earliest memories are of perching on a hassock in front of her while she read the Bible to me or silently to herself, her thin lips forming the words as her knotted, arthritic fingers followed across the page. She explained the stories to me so I could understand and learn to love Jesus.

She taught me other things, too. It was she who taught me to make colored pictures with embrodiery thread. I spent many hours creating flowers and leaves on scarves and pillowcases. Our kitchen towels blossomed from my fingers.

It was left to my mother's sister, however, to try to teach me to play the piano, although my grandmother played "by ear." "It will be better for you to learn to read music," she said. She said the same thing about learning to crochet and knit. "I want you to learn to read the directions," said my retired teacher grandmother. "The discipline will be good for you." Whatever happened to the native talent she had was not passed on to me. Perhaps she took it to the grave with her.

The handwork I managed to master with some degree of skill, but the piano proved a stubborn adversary that I could never control. My dreams were haunted by its bulk. My summer afternoons were sweatily spent glaring at musical notes that I found impossible to translate into sounds that even vaguely resembled music. What pain I must have inflicted on the ears of Aunt Lydia who so faithfully played for services each Sunday. She would flee to the front porch swing with the evening paper, leaving me with the adminition, "Practice makes perfect." So I sweated and fumed.

I do not consider it immature or therapeutic to make such statements. Perhaps what I have needed was the maturity and sense of justice to tell this story. I shall choose a spot and we shall begin.

Chapter 2

Fire! Fire!

There have been some very good novels written from the day of birth of the protagonist, but, in all honesty, I have no baby ideas to recall. I have seen the pictures in the family album. Believe me, they are nothing to brag about. The most outstanding thing about the skinny little kid is the big eyes and ears and little hair. "Isn't he cute," strangers said to my mother when she took me for walks. The old wives' tale said that boys had less hair than baby girls. Maybe they were supposed to have more brains. I was so ugly that I am grateful my parents loved me, or they would have sent me back to wherever I came from and demanded a rebate to boot. Perhaps my looks had something to do with why no more babies came to our house.

"We were married 12 years before you were born," Mamma explained much later. She did not add that five years after my birth she had a complete hysterectomy that threw her directly into menopause. To this day she still has hot flashes.

Although I did not know what operation she had, the day of her return from the hospital is one I will never forget. It was a beautiful Easter Sunday with clear skies and yellow buttercups peeping out of the new grass. That was back when the ill were treated as invalids, and what child would not be impressed when a large white ambulance was backed up to the door? Mamma, pale and looking quite frail, was carried from there to her bed on a stretcher. There she was left "to rest".

The maid put dinner on the table for my father, Aunt Lydia, Uncle Carl and me and then went home to her own Easter celebration. After the meal, my father went to bed because he

4

had to go to work in the mill at 11 that night. The shift at the mill knew no holidays, and the machines and the men and women who ran them worked around the clock all 12 months of the year. For 40 years my father lived an erratic life of 7 to 3 one week, 3 to 11 the next, and then 11 to 7, before repeating the same metabolically confusing process.

In the warm afternoon, my fireman uncle and I walked in the yard. I stopped to indulge in one of my favorite pastimes — watching the mountains as the light changed. At times they looked like the naked arm of a very hairy man. The ridges and rises were like rippling muscles.

A cloud passing would leave dark, hollow spots, like the age spots on an old, old man. The late evening sun would sit on the mountain tops, throwing deep, mysterious shadows where all was quiet. Yes, they were beautiful. I still gain strength from going to the mountains, where I sit quietly, and look at the beauty around me, and let the serenity and peace of the ages soak slowly and surely into my being.

What I saw that afternoon, I thought at first I imagined. It was possible, for I often daydreamed. I made up people of the hills, pioneers in cabins filled with chinks, or Indian campfires for a hunting party to roast fresh killed venison. I blinked, but the smoke was still there, curling into the spring air, disappearing high above the mountain top.

"Look!" I said.

Uncle Carl looked where I was pointing and drew in his breath. "Forest fire," he said, low under his breath. He did not take time to say more, but ran for help.

I was too young to know that the words should have struck terror in me. That is what I would learn before the day was over, as I saw the fire spread, smelled the smoke, and tasted the acrid residue that invaded the senses. I only felt the excitement, as I watched the smoke billow in a larger and larger area.

The men and boys came in cars and trucks. They carried hoes and rakes and shouted in excited voices. "Dag-nab-it Jake, you can't park there. We got to get the equipment through."

"Aw, Henry. We going to have far enough to walk without me parking on the other side of the dad-gum county."

Inside the house, all was cool and quiet. My father and uncle had left. Aunt Lydia sat beside my mother's bed crocheting. "There's no need to be upset, Nellie. The fire's too far away to worry. Carl's in charge and he knows what he's doing. They'll soon have it under control."

I sat in my green wicker rocker in the corner, holding my doll close and reassuring her that Aunt Lydia never lied, and if she said it was so, it was. My nose was filling with an unusual heavy smell. My heart beat faster.

"It's just that the woods are so close," Mamma said. "If that fire gets too close, we'll be in real danger."

I could not sit still. I had to say or do something. I began to understand the meaning of the word fear. This was our home. We lived here as long as I could remember. Nothing must ever destroy that. It was home.

"What can I do to help?" I asked, jumping from my chair and dumping my doll unceremoniously.

"Land sakes, child! You startled me," Aunt Lydia said. Her busy fingers stopped the motion that turned thread into lace, like a spider spins.

"But I want to help," I insisted.

"Why don't you put a few things in the car, in case we need to move your Mamma?" Aunt Lydia suggested, as she picked up her hand work, counting to be sure there were exactly the number of stitches she intended.

I carried things to the car. I do not have any idea what I took. It was something to do and that was better than sitting. Flames mirrored off the blackness and glass of the Cadillac. I did try to put the cat in the car, but he wouldn't stay. He smelled the smoke and felt animal terror at nature out if control.

My fear grew with each trip I made. I looked up at the mountain and could see the smoke getting thicker and closer.

"It's jumped the fire line," I heard one man say, as I passed through the kitchen. He was a man I had never seen before, and yet he sat at our table drinking coffee as though he belonged.

Aunt Lydia busied herself with making coffee and sandwiches. She was tight lipped, unsmiling, and saying little unless spoken to.

A thin man with smudges on his face and something between fear and exhaustion showing in his eyes said, "Yeah, if it would only rain."

"It ain't. It never does when you want it to."

I kept going. I must get as many things as possible in the car. I stopped when Daddy came in looking very weary. He said nothing while I was in the room. I hid around the corner.

"How are things? It doesn't sound too good," Aunt Lydia said.

"It jumped the line."

"I heard that already. Which way's it headed?"

There was a pause and then the rattle of cup on saucer. "It's coming our way, and if we don't get it stopped by night—," he paused.

"Don't think about that. Carl's out there. He's a good fireman." "Yeah, he is," Dad said. "But he's used to fighting in buildings where you can get at the thing, but up there you've got to find it first and when you can get at it, you try to kill it, but it scatters like mercury out of a thermometer."

Aunt Lydia lowered her voice. "Do you guess we ought to get Nellie and B.J. out?"

"Only if we have to." I heard his chair scrape on the floor. "You can't drive, and I can't spare a man."

I didn't wait to hear more but ran through the house as fast as my short legs would carry me. My heart felt like it filled my whole chest. I ran out the front door. The heat from the fire warmed me like August sun. I ran down the steps. This awful thing was not happening. Surely this was a bad dream.

At the house nearest us, I could see two women working. One was on the roof and the other was handing up soaked tow sacks from a galvanized tub on the ground. Nearby I saw Grandpa Alder, who was the oldest man I knew. He was raking twigs and leaves as far away from the house as he could. I had never seen him move so fast, and where was his cane?

I could not stand to watch. With tears running down my face, I ran around the corner of the house. I don't know where the cat came from, but one minute I was running hell-bent-for-leather and the next I was on the ground with gravel and dirt making bloody patches on my knees and hands. I was under Mamma's

7

window and I could hear her scream, "Ly-dah! Ly-dah! Go see about the child!"

The cat took off, his tail a rudder in his wake.

Then I cried in great body-shaking sobs. It made me feel better. When you see blood it's all right to cry. That is the way you deal with pain, cry. Then someone would come and wash your sores and put on Mercurochrome, which didn't hurt, instead of Iodine, which burned.

"My word," Aunt Lydia said, as she ran to me wiping her hands on her apron. "Here, here, now. Put your arms around my neck. I'll take care of you."

It was when she picked me up that I saw flames licking the distant tree tops. I gasped in wide-eyed terror. It was the end. My safe world was gone.

I cried and screamed, my body going stiff. Aunt Lydia struggled until she got me into the kitchen. I did not see the blow coming, but I felt its sting as my head snapped back. I gasped but stopped yelling. I calmed down and remembered I was not a baby anymore.

"Hush up, B.J. You just hush. You'll upset your Mamma." She opened her mouth to tell me I ought to be ashamed not to put my sick mother first, but the shrill voice came from Mamma's room.

"Now see what you've done," Aunt Lydia said, putting me firmly on a stool. "You stay right there until I get back."

I stayed, feeling miserable that I had been so selfish. Now I could hear the fire roar like a beast from hell. A man's voice called, "Need more men over here."

Aunt Lydia came back. "Land-a-Goshen, and don't I have my hands full? A sick woman, an hysterical child, to say nothing of men trooping across the clean floor in dirty boots while the whole world burns outside." As she talked, she cleaned me up and got the iodine. I was too terrified of what I heard outside to object. What was that about the kitchen floor? Soon there would be no house, much less kitchen floor. I began to giggle.

This time she shook me by the shoulders. "You stop that. You can't have any more spells, you hear?"

I tried but between the giggles and my snubbing I had the hiccoughs.

"Here," Aunt Lydia said, handing me a glass of water. "Hold your nose and drink this. How much more am I supposed to put up with today?"

While I drank the water no hiccoughs, but when I handed her the glass they began again. I giggled an apology.

"That's all right, B.J." she said. "You just laugh right on. You'll need a sense of humor to get along in this old world," and then she turned, jumped half-way across the floor and hollered, "Boo!"

I nearly fell off the stool, but the hiccoughs did not stop.

"Well, I declare," she said, holding her chin in her hand. "I don't know but one other thing to do." She handed me a lunch bag. "Here, blow in this."

I took the bag and tried to concentrate on the task, but there was something on the periphery of my mind and it took me a few minutes to realize what it was. I put the bag down.

"What is it, child?"

"Listen," I said with tears coming. All we heard was silence. In the distance a dog barked. The cat purred at the door wanting dinner.

"I don't hear anything," Aunt Lydia said.

"I don't either," I cried jumping from the stool into her arms.

We ran to the door together.

"By God, I think we got it, Leroy," we heard one man call.

"We sure as hell have," another replied.

Aunt Lydia and I laughed and cried and turned in circles. Oh, the joy of being alive and without fear of having your whole life torn apart!

We ran in to tell mother the wonderful news, but backed off when we saw she was asleep.

Most of the weary men went home that night, knowing what they had to be grateful for. Some of them stayed through the night to be sure the fire did not break out again.

This story may seem a strange place to begin, but it is not, for it was with the fire that I began to learn. There are no sure bets in this world, no lifetime guarantees.

Chapter 3

My Uncle Jerome

I said in the beginning that I was going to write about myself, and so I am, but the fact is I am a story teller. The fact is, this is a novel. Therefore, I tell a story based, along the way, on some facts. How much is fact and how much fiction only I know for sure. This is not an apology but only to clarify that this is not an autobiography, nor is it intended to reveal all of me, but it is a story to bring order out of chaos. In fact, it is the magnificent lie.

All children are affected by the world around them, and I was no different. My world however, was peopled with adults, when there were people at all. Much of my childhood was spent alone. I learned to love books, my pets, and to trust my imagination. I learned early the difference between being alone and being lonely. Perhaps I was, even then, in training to be a writer.

There were certain people who captured my attention. Two people stand out in my memory because they fit no mold that I was familiar with. Uncle Jerome and Aunt Hilda came home for Christmas every two or three years. They always arrived in a big black car. Slightly built Uncle Jerome, with his black hair and red satin shirt, sat behind the wheel, while rosy-cheeked, white-haired Aunt Hilda sat beside him with the road map in her lap.

"Hot dang, did I ever play a joke on the Pope," Uncle Jerome said. "I promised before I married Hilda that we'd bring our kids up Catholic.'' He threw his head back and laughed. His laugh was contagious. "I knew dang good and well there weren't going to be any children.''

Aunt Hilda was second generation German and spoke English as a second language. Home to her was Minnesota, which she pronounced as "Minn-e-sot-a.'' She was devoted to work and cleanliness. She would put Uncle Jerome in the galvanized tub she used to bathe her own children. She would scrub behind his ears and he would cuss. "Dag-nab-it, woman. You're rubbing my skin off.''

I can see him now as clearly as I did then, that great uncle of mine. He drank too much. He gambled and cussed and loved a good joke. Oh, how he laughed. He laughed at what the rest of my world took all too seriously. "Why in the pluperfect hell does a man have to get up early in the morning if he doesn't have cows to milk?'' he complained about my grandfather's early rising habits. Uncle Jerome made this statement while standing in front of my grandmother's cook stove, warming his behind. His hair was tousled. His suspenders sagged around his hips and the top button of his BVD's was undone.

"Because this is my house,'' my grandfather roared, looking over his glasses. "And when I get up, everybody gets up.''

Uncle Jerome cursed, ending the conversation. He was a little man, but I saw him as the biggest man in the world, standing there in his sock feet. He was the only person I knew willing to take on my dictatorial grandfather.

"Never trust a man who won't look you in the eye, B.J.,'' Uncle Jerome told me. He always looked me in the eye, and he never talked down to me. I learned a lot from him. He told tales so grand that there was no way to believe them. He also loved practical jokes. "When your Mamma and Aunt Lydia were little girls, I told them to get every chair in the house and stack them to the ceiling and I would take off my shoes and step over them. Bet'em a nickel I could do it too.''

"Did they do it?'' I asked, second guessing what was coming.

"Dang tootin, they did.''

"Let me guess. Let me guess.''

His blue eyes twinkled. "Go on and guess then.''

"You took off your shoes and stepped over THEM.''

11

"You little booger," he said, punching me affectionately on the shoulder. "You know your old uncle pretty well, don't you?"

"Did you make Mamma and Aunt Lydia pay up?"

"They were just kids, but I made their mamma pay. A nickel's a nickel."

I was ready for him when we were playing cards and he wanted to see my hand. I showed him my hand but not my cards. It was from these games that I learned to think fast and smart.

I could tell by his eyes and the wrinkles around them when he told me the truth and when he lied. I studied his face. I watched his hands that were seldom still, and I learned from him that people do not have to play games unless they choose to. If I forget, I can hear his voice in the back of my mind. "Hot dang, B.J., you've done it again!"

"You really ought to have those red shoes," he said in the shoe department of Grants.

Oh how I wanted them. "Mamma will pay you back," I lied, looking him square in the eyes. I knew good and well she wouldn't. I'd be lucky if she let me wear them outside of the house.

"Since you and I are both gamblers, B.J., I guess we'll just take the risk," he said, pulling his wallet from his hip pocket. It was a little frightening to know he'd read my mind.

"B.J. really pulled a good one, Nellie," he laughed. I was not only trapped but betrayed. "Put your money away, Nellie," he said, giving me a wink. "And you don't lay a hand on her either. She's smart. You leave her alone." It seemed that my education was worth more than a nickel.

"And right there in the hall they cut the man's leg off," he said from his deathbed. "His screams were awful." The opiates that eased his physical pain, sent him into horrible imaginings where monsters roamed and men had their legs cut off without anesthetic. He was dying and I could not save him, but I can be what he taught me and so I come to these pages with truths and lies. I know the difference but no one else does, unless he looks into my eyes. There truth is open and undisguised.

12

Chapter 4

The Funeral

Handling grief is a very personal thing. Some people cry loudly, scream and tear at their clothes like they used to at old-fashioned funerals. Boy, did I ever attend a lot of them in my childhood. I remember being squeezed between two adults and being warned that the wrath of God would be on my head if I dared breathe too loud.

The country church funerals were the worst. If the dead person had been a suicide or been murdered, the church and yard were sure to be filled with those both sympathetic and curious. When Joe Faircloth was killed in an argument over a woman who was what was called behind cupped hands, a "loose woman," he had a grand sending off. The small clapboard church was located in one of the far corners of the county. We rode as far as Vale Hollow on the main road. There we turned left toward the mountains and went as far as the road went, which was into the front of a dilapidated store. From there we turned onto a very rutted road that was wide enough for approximately 1½ cars. If we met another car, somebody had to back up.

I sat on the front seat of the car sandwiched between my mother and father. My father was a very handsome man with high cheekbones, brown curly hair and gray eyes. We looked more like the three bears than people. My father wore a gray felt hat with the brim snappily tilted. Over his blue tweed suit he wore his overcoat. I peeped at him occasionally to admire his profile. Mother wore a black hat with a turned up brim and her gray karakul fur coat. Oh, how I loved that coat with the soft curly fur that caressed the fingertips. I sat between them, with my short legs sticking out in front of me. In addition to my underwear, I wore a dress, a sweater, a heavy coat, leggings, socks, shoes and overshoes. Around my neck was a scarf and on my head was my tweed cap with ear flaps, to say nothing of the wool gloves on my hands. The heater was running full blast. I was sweating. Virginia may be a part of the Sunny South, but it got damn cold where I came from.

"Looks like it might snow," Daddy said.

"I hope not before the service is over. It's so sad to bury anybody in bad weather," Mamma replied.

Daddy grunted. "Now, Nellie, we have no control over those things."

"How many children did you say he had?"

"Five."

"Humph! And him out tom-catting around with that old rip."

"Nellie, the child." We rode on in silence.

Mamma spoke up. "How long did you work with him?"

"Maybe 10 years. Maybe more." That was more years than I was old. The dead man must have been very old. Why, he might be as much as 25 or so.

Our first whiff of the outside air was a searing jet that went in icicle-cold and came out in puffs like dragon smoke. The ground underfoot gave only a little under the pressure of our feet.

The small church was already half-filled when we got there. It was one square room with green, beaded walls and ceiling. The brown wooden benches stood as though frozen to the floor. They well night have been, for there was one pot-bellied stove to heat the room and, at the front of the church, the doors stood wide, letting in people and cold air. A lectern had been moved to one side to make room for the flowers and casket with its open lid.

"You going to see him?" Mamma asked.

14

"I thought you might remember him if you saw," Daddy replied, taking her by the arm.

I was guided to where the casket stood. I was not tall enough to see.

"I'm still not sure I remember him," Mamma said.

The flowers were beautiful. If there is one thing that does not change, it is the smell of funeral flowers. In my mind, gladiola's and mums mean funerals. But I have other, better memories of both. In summer, Mamma used to arrange huge vases of orange and white glads from the yard, placing them on the buffet where the back of the arrangement was reflected in the long mirror.

I had several mum corsages for the football games. Somewhere I still have the ribbons, hidden away, never looked at. I was brought up to save things. That must be the reason for there is no need to keep such things in an age when football games clutter my den every Saturday and Sunday from August through the next January.

We were seated. First was Mother, then me, and Daddy nearest the aisle. That was in the old days when men still believed in the chivalrous acts. My father was such a man. He walked on the curb side of the sidewalk. Until he died, he opened doors and held chairs. It was part of his charm.

When the church was filled with people, and some were overflowing to the outside, a woman with a false gardenia on her hat sat at the upright piano and played. Not only was the piano out of tune, but the woman must have learned to play wearing boxing gloves.

The worst was yet to come as two women stood to sing. The soprano was tall. The alto was fat. After attacking "Crossing The Bar," they turned their attention to "The Old Rugged Cross." It did not occur to me at the time to be critical. I knew that in a country church, a choir was not easy to come by. Anyone willing to try to sing was welcome. I used to sing in one of those choirs; I ought to know.

The last to arrive was the family. It was pitiful. The wife was supported on either side by pale-faced young men. She was dressed in black from head to foot, including a

15

veil. Her sobs were heard before she could be seen.

Mamma pinched me on the knee when I tried to turn around to look. "That's not nice," she hissed in my ear.

All of the man's family followed, and there were many of them. I guessed a white-haired lady with a flushed face must have been his mother. It was hard to tell which children were the dead man's and which were not.

Slowly the family went by the casket for a last look at a face they had taken for granted for so long. The wife collapsed and had to be carried to her seat. "No! No!" she said over and over again.

I slid my glove off and pressed my hand into the softness of mother's fur coat between the sleeve and her side. How could anyone endure the pain that woman was going through? I looked from my mother to my father. Could I stand to undergo such a terrible thing? My heart ached and tears ran down my cheeks. Those poor children, those poor, poor children.

There were two preachers. The prayers were long, giving me a chance to nod off as I got warm from my snuggled position. The minister's words were many. After a while I did not even try to listen. The sobbing woman on the front row and my inner thoughts were much more interesting.

My grandmother sat me near her in the sitting room. "I think that you ought to know about your father, B.J., because I know you love him."

"Yes, ma'am." I replied, not being able to imagine what she was going to say, yet knowing by the seriousness of her voice that this was important.

"I don't know whether you realize it or not, but your father is not a well man." It would be years before I learned to be leery of any statement that followed that three-letter word "but." She put her hand on mine. "I don't know whether you understand what I am trying to tell you or not. Your father may not be with us for long."

My mouth fell open. I could feel the tears coming.

"You are a very sensitive child, and I would not want you to live to have any regrets."

16

"I'll be good to him, Grandma. I'll be good. I love Daddy." And then I dissolved into tears.

I lived with the spectre of my father's death for a very long time. Grandma was right. He did die, in 1976, at age 80, many years after she was gone.

On that long ago, cold, blustery day when that man was lowered into the ground, I knew only that one day my father would lie in such a grave. I was miserable. I can and do borrow great quantities of empathy. It is a handicap sometimes, and I have learned to draw away for objectivity toward life.

Chapter 5

The Other Side Of
The Family Tree

It was a bitter cold evening and already dark outside. I lay with my cheek rubbing the soft bearskin rug. Despite the roaring fire in the huge old fireplace, my feet were cold. My cousins sat at a nearby table reading the Sunday supplement of "The Washington Post" and "The New York Times" we had brought them. There was Dick Tracy, Smiling Jack, and Andy Gump.

From the next room came the clatter of pans as Aunt Zella prepared dinner. The sound of her voice, as well as that of my mother's came to me. Although they were both Virginians, their accents were very different. My mother's voice had the muted Piedmont drawl while my aunt's had the distinctive mountain turn that flattened vowels. The sound of the two women talking was almost music.

The sound was accented by the smell of pinto beans, almost done, and cornbread. You could just starve thinking about it. My 4-year-old mouth watered.

A kerosene lamp flickered on the round table where my cousins sat poring over the papers. Occasionally, one would laugh or say, "Well, look here."

The comfort of lying there so warm and listening to the wind whistle in the eaves was lulling. I almost fell asleep.

18

The door flew open with a bang. A gust of wind made the lamp flicker. My father and my uncle came in, stamping snow from their feet.

From my position in front of the fire, both men seemed colossal. The two men took off their coats. My father wore an overcoat and my uncle, his brother, a sheepskin lined coat. The metal clasps on Uncle Robert's heavy boots clanged as he walked.

Daddy sat on the cane bottomed chair next to the fireplace and took off his rubber galoshes. "It's the wind that makes it so cold," he said.

"Supper's ready," Aunt Zella called.

I was so comfortable, I hated to move. I'd rather be there in that farmhouse with its drafts and rattling windows than anyplace on earth.

My cousins did not have to be called twice. They had all been in school that day in the clapboard one room school across the road where they huddled as near the pot-bellied stove as they were permitted. I had been allowed to go with them for a half day and I knew how eager each of them was to recite so he could go to the front of the class and stand between the teacher's desk and the stove. It was never really warm in the room because there was no electricity in the entire county and no blower on the stove to circulate the air. Even if there had been, the building, which sat several feet off the ground, had no underpinning, and no insulation. If the wind didn't chill your bones by blowing side to side, it did up and down.

Of course, when my cousins got home from school, they had chores to do. The boys had to chop and bring in wood for the cookstove and the fireplace. They also had to feed the cows, pigs, horses, and sheep. The older ones had to milk the cows. The girls had to clean and fill the lamps, feed the chickens, gather the eggs, and, when they were old enough, help with the cooking. They also had to bring the water from the springhouse and wash the dishes. There was no danger of the devil finding idle minds to get into mischief on that working farm.

We were all seated around the long oil-cloth covered table with much scraping of chairs. Spoons rattled coffee cups. Milk glasses were filled from an earthenware pitcher. Cornbread was

19

broken, never sliced. "It makes it sad," the old saying was . The food was simple and wholesome. There was always plenty of it.

After dinner, when the dishes were clean and put in their proper places in the cupboard and the dishpan hung on a nail beside the door, the family gathered in front of the fire. My cousins put away the papers and got out their school books. The older ones were stopped in their own work from time to time to help a younger brother or sister.

Aunt Zella sat in her rocker with a lap full of socks to be darned. Money was scarce, and every piece of clothing was patched and darned carefully. Everyone knew there was no shame in being poor as long as you were clean. After all, cleanliness is next to godliness.

Daddy leaned back in his chair with his feet stretched toward the fire. "Mighty fine meal, Zella." Although Daddy usually spoke with no trace of his orgins, except for certain words such as "nice" and "knife," it only took him a few hours to revert to his native dialect when he was there.

Uncle Robert leaned forward and poked the log with the poker. He was a bigger man than my father, with the ruddy complexion of a man who spent most of his time out of doors. He had a shock of white hair and eyes so blue that he could look right through you if he wanted to. I was not afraid of him but I was in awe. I'm not sure if it was his size or his gruffness that made me believe he was God.

"When are you going to join the church?" Mamma asked.

He poked at the log again. "Well, Nellie," he said "I reckon I'll just wait until I'm on my deathbed and then confess." He spat tobacco juice into the fire. "That's what's called covering your bets. Any man worth his salt knows there's no such thing as God, anyway." He pushed his cap to the back of his head. He was the only man I knew who wore his hat in the house. "I've never asked for a thing I didn't work for and I'm not going to start now." There was no argument. It would have been a waste of breath.

Everyone went to bed early. We children climbed the narrows steps to the second floor, led by the glow of the lamp one cousin carried. The opening of the door at the top of the stairs let in a blast of freezing air. The upstairs was not heated. In winter it was bitter cold. In summer you sweltered there under the tin roof that popped and cracked as it cooled in the night air.

Our breath puffed in front of us like balloons over cartoon character's heads. It did not take us long to shed our clothes and don our flannel pajamas.

I will never forget that bed. For one thing, it was painted bright purple. That, in itself, should have kept us warm.

On the bed was a feather bed topped by mounds of quilts. If you have never slept in a feather bed, you have missed a treat. You sink down, down, down like sinking in clouds. The bed rises around you and folds over you like the arms of a mother. The air might sting your nose but you were warm and you slept the sleep of the righteous.

Years later, when I was grown, I was talking to Uncle Robert and I told him that I had thought he was God when I was little.

He threw his head back and laughed. "By God, you might of been right."

This man of flesh and bone, with a steel trap for a soul, lived well into his 90s and he never did let anyone tell him what to do. One of his ideas was that a bathroom belonged in the back yard, not in the house. "It's not nice to do that in the house," he said.

They got electricity and water in the house and a telephone. Even when he was quite old and feeble and there was a bathroom in the house he refused to use it except to shave.

Daddy's other brothers and sisters we saw occasionally. One of the things I remember vividly was all of the good food. Each household had a specialty. One aunt made hot potato salad and stack cakes with mounds of raspberry jam. Another made banana pies that literally melted in your mouth. All served mounds of fried chicken with milk gravy and fried ham with red-eyed. Platters were heaped with ears of corn and there were side dishes of green beans cooked with ham hock, and bowls of fluffy creamed potatoes. Both biscuits and cornbread were served with home-churned butter. Desserts were plentiful and rich, with all washed down with strong steaming coffee and all the fresh milk you could drink. When you worked as hard as these people did, it took a lot of food to keep you going.

It was not until later that I realized that much of my poor but proud relative's time was spent in providing the food that went

21

on their tables. They had something, however, that many people more affluent did not have. They had each other and they grew and blossomed in the light of each other's love.

One summer I spent two weeks with my cousins who lived besides the river. It was a broad shallow river whose sound sang you to sleep at night. The house was small. Painted white on the outside, and kept neat on the inside, it was a good place to be.

"I like it when you're here, B.J." my cousin Catherine said.

"You do?"

"Yes," she said raking her barefoot in the dust. "When you're here, I don't have to work so hard."

I had learned long before that my cousins spent a large part of their summers working beside their parents on the farm. They hoed and gathered vegetables and helped store the food that would see them through the hard mountain winters.

Daddy always had a garden, but he tended it himself. As one person said. "Albert's garden is cleaner than my house." He was good and he was meticulous. "A green thumb is really a brown back," Daddy always said.

Life on the farm, however, was not all work. My uncle had a flat-bottomed boat, and on a hot afternoon we were allowed to float down the river. Tom Sawyer had nothing on us. On the way to the boat we would stop at the grape vines that grew on the front fence and pull bunches of big purple grapes. From the boat you could look down in the water and see fish scurrying along over the rocks of the river bottom. Our laughter bounced back to us off the cliff walls on the other side of the river.

My uncle also had a horse. When he was not using the horse to plow, we were allowed to ride him. I loved horses but most of my knowledge about them came from books. I had read "Black Beauty," "My Friend Flicka," "Thunderhead," and I had seen "National Velvet" but the sheer joy of riding was new to me. It may have been just a farm work horse, but to me it was Buttermilk, I was Dale Evans and I was, "back in the saddle again."

On Saturday night my cousins and I scrubbed behind our ears, put on our best clothes and squeezed into the front of the pickup truck. We went to a camp meeting.

The tent sat in the middle of a field with its sides rolled up. A generator hummed beside one pole and pale light shown from bare light bulbs strung around the inside of the tent like Christmas tree lights.

On the ground surrounding the tent cars and trucks were parked. One car had one wheel higher than the others because it was on a rock. A truck near where we parked had hissing from a tire.

There were people of all ages milling about. A pregnant young woman with a little boy on her hip fanned herself with a folded piece of newspaper. A hump-backed old woman with snow-white hair swung a cane in her right hand as she shuffled along.

"Let's sit at the back so we can see everything," Catherine suggested.

A bald-headed man elbowed by us. He was so heavy that he was panting for breath.

"He'd better get religion," Catherine said. "As fat as he is, he'll meet his maker soon enough."

I nodded agreement, as we sat on the back bench. There were no chairs but wood benches without backs.

A woman about halfway down the aisles caught my attention. It was impossible to tell whether the lines on her face were from age or hard work. She had attempted to pull her dingy hair into a bun at the nape of her neck but wisps had escaped and hung limply around her pale face. The corners of her mouth were pulled down as though despair had taken her over and would never let her smile again. Her thin shoulders sagged and she might have been any number of other people there but for one thing. She wore a frayed black coat with a worn collar.

"Who is that woman?" I asked.

Catherine shrugged, "Which one?"

"That one."

"Her?" Catherine said and rolled her eyes skyward. "That's Ruby Jones, and we don't talk about her."

"Why?" I asked. My curiosity was peeked.

Catherine tapped her forehead. "A bit draft."

I nodded that I understood when I wasn't really sure I did.

The music was provided by an ancient out-of-tune piano and a tambourine manned by the preacher. Even with the tent sides up, the closeness of the bodies soon made the main odor in the air sweat. If the music was bad, and it was, the preaching was worse. There are some people who have to be shouted into heaven; I am not one.

İ had been to tent meetings before, but what happened that night was beyond anything I had seen before. First, an old man in overalls started to scream, "Lord Jesus, Lord Jesus! I hear you calling my name."

Next, a young girl stood and started flailing her arms in the air. I could not understand her. "What is she saying?" I asked.

"She's speaking in tongues," Catherine said.

I watched wide-eyed until suddenly Ruby Jones jumped into the middle of the aisle and started jumping up and down as she twirled like a whirling dervish. I was startled and then as I watched closely, I became amused and then laughed so hard the tears came.

Ruby Jones was not only wearing a black coat with only one button at the throat but galoshes in black with none of the snaps fastened. As she jumped up and down, the coat and boots flapped, making a very loud noise of whoosh-clack, whoosh-clack. She might have been the devil's own angel making comment on the proceedings except she kept saying over and over, "Dear God! Dear God!"

I had to get out of there. The cool night air might have brought me to my senses if one of my cousins hadn't said every mile or so, "Oh, God! Oh, God!

All of that was a long time ago, but I learned some things that have been important in my life. You don't have to be rich to be important to those who love you.

Chapter 6

Trying To Conform

"Are you really sure?" I asked. My heart beat faster. I was in the process of making a decision. I was a child, and children were supposed to do as they were told. Why, I even took afternoon naps until I started to school. I thought everybody did.

"Yes," my friend replied, bobbing her pigtails. "We're even having chicken for supper." Everybody knew you had chicken for Sunday dinner or when you had company. I was expected to come home from school with my friend. If you were expected to do something, you did.

That is how I came to be on a different school bus, and how I came to be in someone else's house for cookies and milk. We did have chicken for dinner. Later my friend and I sat at the dining room table with our books open in front of us. We were probably doing more giggling than working when there was a knock at the door. It was my father. My pleasure in seeing him was short-lived. He stopped by the side of the road on the way home and spanked me, for "scaring your mother half to death."

For years I lived under the cloud of being a thoughtless person, of shaming myself as disobedient, and as not being reliable. After all, who would trust a child who went home with a friend just because she wanted to? Now I could meet some old classmates and this fiasco would be all they remember. My real crime, of course, was in doing what I wanted instead of conforming to what others expected of me.

25

Disobedience was not really my most common offense. In fact, I was very eager to please. I brought my mother flowers. I said, "Yes, m'am", and called my elders "sir."

One of my great problems was an occasional lie. I felt justified in my fabrications, for they were for the purpose of protecting myself. As well as I remember, the lies did not help me get away without a spanking, but they did postpone a few. My father hated a liar and really laid it on me when he caught me.

My hair was cut very short and I wore huge hairbows on one side. They were beautiful ribbons of taffeta and ranged in colors of the rainbow. I liked the bows but hated the haircut. I also hated my clothes. For one thing, I was the only kid in my class who wore store-bought clothes. My mother couldn't sew and, after all, there was a war on. I longed for a dress made out of feed sacks like those of my classmates.

That was not the worst part, however. My mother insisted that a small girl like me was really adorable when her skirt was short enough for all the world to see the lace on her panties. What agonies I went through trying to keep my skirt pulled down. No matter how hard I tried, that skirt would come only half-way down my thighs in front, and oh! the cold shock I got when I sat in a desk seat on a winter Monday morning! I was also sneered at. "Who wants to play with somebody with no clothes on?"

It was a spring day when we grammar school girls were all gathered into the fifth-grade classroom for a talk on fashions. I thought the teacher who gave the talk was the prettiest I had ever seen. She was tall, with long blonde hair and very blue eyes. I'll bet she was even a pretty little girl and not drab like me. Best of all, she dressed in style. I would daydream about being all grown up and wearing clothes like hers. No one else I knew dressed so well. When I grew up, I wanted to be a classy looking lady like that teacher.

I do not remember what she said, but I do remember that I was feeling more and more miserable. There seemed no place in the world for a mouse like me, and there seemed to be nothing I could do about it.

"And ladies," she said in conclusion. People always call young girls 'ladies' and old ladies 'girls' when they want to make them feel good. "The length of ladies' dresses is going down this spring."

Now there was something for me to think about. If ladies dresses were getting longer, then so would those of my classmates. I was unhappy then, and things would get worse. Why shouldn't I at least have my skirt longer, if only by the width of a hem? I tugged and pulled until I had all the threads loose. I felt beautiful.

Until I got home. "What happened to your beautiful dress? It's obvious it is not torn. You're going to tell me, B.J. What happened? You're going to tell me."

My ears roared. I had not thought far enough ahead to face this. My heart pounded. What could I say? I was really going to get it this time.

"You'd better not lie to me. What happened?"

I bit the inside of my lip. My throat was dry. I could feel the tears coming.

"Well, B.J., I'm waiting."

And then I opened my mouth and there was the lie. "The teacher made me do it." It was so obvious that even I didn't believe it.

"Your teacher?"

I dared not open my betraying mouth again. I nodded.

"Indeed! I don't know what these teachers think they're doing these days. If they'd teach like they're supposed to, they wouldn't have time for anything else." She paused for breath.

I was really crying. The teacher I admired the most might get in trouble because of me. I was miserable.

"Was it a man or woman?" she asked. I didn't know why that mattered.

"Woman," I answered. At least that was the truth. I could guess what the next question would be. She knew all of the teachers.

"I think I'll just call that school and give them a piece of my mind."

The story is not over here. I got the spanking and the preaching and scorn at school, too. I also continued to wear the

27

short dresses.

My worst offense, however, was my temper. "Ladies don't fight," I was told. What I learned was that the smallest kid in the group got beat up when she did fight. I had no brothers or sisters to defend me. I probably had my chin stuck out with "hit here" tatooed on it. It was always my gloves that got thrown out of the bus window and my lunch that was ground into the floor. It was pure luck that I was allowed to ride the bus rather than run along behind it.

"Whose book is this?"

"Why, I do believe it belongs for B.J."

"Can I have a page?"

"What for? You can't read."

Amid the laughter, I was trying to get my book. Big Red, in the sixth grade, by the Grace of God and tired teachers, at the age of sixteen, was holding me at arm's length with the palm of his hand. His fingers were tangled in my hair, and trying to get away only resulted in sharp yanks.

"B.J., what you going to do if we tear up that book?"

I flailed both fists in the air, hitting nothing. I loathed those boys. Tears made everything swim like mirages. "Give me my book. It's mine."

"Give her, her book, Leroy. It's hers," one mocked.

I struck out again. I tried to kick but had no better luck.

"It's hers. It's hers," they chanted. I heard the page tear. My anger turned to fury. I jerked away from Big Red and plunged into what had to be defeat, but I got in some blows.

When it was over, Big Red helped me to my feet. My nose was bleeding and I had a sore cheek. I held the torn book in my hand. He said, "Gees, B.J., I never thought this was going to happen. Your mamma's really going to raise Cain now." He helped me to my gate, but not even Big Red was willing to face what I would have to.

That was only one time my temper got me in over my head. It took me years to control my anger. I taught myself to look at all sides of a question and try to understand. I forced myself to smile when I seethed inside. Much later I began to wonder, "Why don't you have a right to show anger like everybody else?" That soul search led to the conclusion that any ground I stand on is my turf and anybody who steps on my toes had better be ready to fight.

The ones I learned to dislike most were the self-righteous who knew just how everybody should live. They were the many, and I was different. With my mountain father and my Southern lady mother, there was no way they could make me see as they did. My toes were turned away from them and beyond my bloody nose. You wait! I thought.

Chapter 7

Pets Who Have Known Me

None of the complications I experienced in dealing with people affected another part of my growing up. My pets asked only to be fed, scratched behind the ears and loved.

There were always cats and dogs at the house. "You can't have just one kitten. The poor little thing would get lonesome and, besides, they are so cute when they play together." I believed this because I wanted to. Since we lived next to a busy highway, they didn't last long, necessitating a pet cemetery. I held funerals for my loves and sang hymns over their crushed bones and prayed their pitiful souls into animal heaven.

Not all of the pets died an untimely death. Billy was a big red and white Persian. His body, and, in particular, his ears, were scarred and bruised from his many romantic battles. He was quite a Romeo. His adventures sometimes took him miles from home, so it was not unusual for him to be gone for weeks. One time he left us and did not come back.

"Dear B.J., Billy has come home. He has been to college and now he's home. He's and old man now and mostly sleeps by the fire." The letter came in my freshman year at college. As nearly as we could tell, someone had carried him off and he had spent a year and a half trying to get home when he wandered onto a local college campus. A kind lady took him in. "He was a mess when I got him," she said. "His fur was matted, and his feet were so sore he could hardly walk." When Christmas holidays came, the woman could no longer keep him. A mutual friend knew we always kept pets and got in touch with my parents.

It was like seeing a reincarnated friend to see Billy again. He was thinner, older, and perhaps smarter, but this friend of my childhood was home. Our joy was short-lived, for he died before spring.

Some of the cats were not with us long. My uncle told us about two black kittens. "They're solid black and a little wild because they've been raised around a barn. They'll calm down, though."

Mamma and I went to get our new kittens. As promised, they were solid black with eyes like emeralds. Long and lean half-grown cats peeped out of the box with hate in their eyes. Like sleek panthers they crouched.

When we got home, we took the box to the middle of the living room floor. Pandora never unleashed two such evils on the unsuspecting world. Two streaks flew from the box. They clawed the furniture, climbed the table legs, scaled the drapes and leapt across the width of the room with claws extended. All the while they spat, hissed, and yowled obscenities inherited from their jungle forefathers.

I stood rooted to the spot in stark horror. Never in my wildest dreams did I ever imagine such demons.

Mamma got the broom. One cat was bowed on top of the radio from which he had sent the nut bowl flying with pecans, walnuts, and Brazil nuts scattered in all directions. Mamma slipped first one way and then the other as nuts cracked or slid under her feet. Her arms flailed, the broom dangled in her hand.

The other cat slid across an end table, knocking pictures and a vase in all directions. The vase broke. Cat-claw marks ate through the dark varnish and into the wood.

"Open the door," Mamma yelled above the catterwauling.

The last time we saw them, they were two black behinds running out the door with tails like flags in the breeze. No one had to tell me after that that a wild animal cannot be tamed.

Daddy was very good with folk medicines and often brought hurt wild animals home. One time there was a red fox with a paw wounded in a trap. Daddy warned me, "It's all right for you to go look, B.J., but don't ever forget he's wild. He doesn't know, or care what your intentions are."

I squatted on the rise opposite his cage, right in the middle of the forget-me-not bed. He was magnificent. The red fur rolled over his muscular body as he moved. His gold eyes watched my every move. I watched his. He paced back and forth. I sat very still on my haunches. I smiled. If only I could touch him. Soon he stopped pacing, sat and eyed me. I did not lose eye contact, but I also noticed his markings. There has to be a God. No artist could so perfectly mark an animal.

"You afraid?" I whispered.

He flicked one ear. It was hard to tell if he heard me or if there was a fly. It was late in the year for a fly.

"You're beautiful, you know that?" I asked.

He squinched both eyes. Did he understand? If only he could talk.

We sat quietly eyeing each other. He yawned. I sighed. "Well," I said, still talking low. "Mr. Fox," I said with due respect, "I reckon I better go."

He did not stand up but perked his ears to attention. "I hope you feel better tomorrow, with that sore foot and all." I got up and started away. I had another thought and turned to speak to him. He was pacing again. "Mr. Fox, I said."I'm pleased to meet you,"

However brief this encounter, it taught me to respect beauty.

Not all of the pets were either cats or wild animals. There was a succession of dogs, mostly Daddy's hunting dogs. There were Tillies and Jakes always. "You stay away from the dog. A good hunting dog is not a pet," Daddy told me.

One dog was a pet, however. Lulu was a fox terrier, and she had all of us wrapped around her paw. A family rule was that dogs were not to be inside the house, and yet Lulu spent most of each winter behind the cook stove. "But she was cold, Nellie," Daddy would say if Mamma complained.

Two of my favorite pets were a pair of kids named Snowwhite and Sneezy. There is something charming about two bleating, knobbykneed, black-eyed creatures who would sneak up behind you and do their best to knock you flat.

No one told me that Daddy was getting rid of the goats until the deed was done. "Yeh, he sold them to the man at the junk yard," my uncle said. "And he's eating them for supper." I believed him and knew what a broken heart was. What a horror for my babies! What an ignoble end! It was not so.

There was one pet, not mine, I would gladly have seen in anybody's stew. He was Jim Crow and no friend of mine. One of my chores was to clean the front porch. We had wicker furniture with cotton stuffed cushions. That bird kept our porch covered with cotton and stole the buttons off the cushions. He was also a pro at stealing clothes pins off the line. He was loud, brassy, and a thorough pest.

He really got me on a Sunday morning. I was dressed up, including one of my big hairbows. I had just read a comic book the night before in which a condor swooped down and carried people off to his nest high in the mountains. Down swooped old Jim Crow and landed right on top of my head, claws extended. I knew I was a goner. My blood curdling scream could probably be heard in the next county. I don't know who was scared the worst, me or old Jim. Here came Mamma to the rescue with her trusty broom. To save me, I could feel no remorse when someone shot Jim.

There were many pets in my childhood. Since a lot of my time was spent alone, they were very important to me. They were easy to love and very hard to give up when something happened to them. I learned the valuable lesson that to live brings pain as well as pleasure.

Chapter 8

Travel Broadens

"Travel broadens," the old saw goes. If you do much of it, there is one part of the anatomy sure to show the effects.

Mamma liked to travel. Daddy did not, and because he worked shift work at the mill, he was seldom with us on a trip. The exception was his yearly trip to Chesapeake Bay to go deep sea fishing. Mother and I usually went with him. Mamma had absolutely no interest in fishing and had no intention of getting on a boat. She could get sick driving across a bridge over six inches of water. I wanted to go with Daddy. I loved the sound of the lapping water, and the smell. the glint of the sun, like tin foil, off the water made me squint. The excitement I felt inside had no name. I was simply reacting to that foreign environment. I could imagine strange worlds on the other side of the body of water. That feeling came back to me years later, when I sat on the grass at the seaside at Skeeries, Ireland. The sea gulls and terns chattering, the sand and sea smell I loved all seemed familiar. Peace came over my soul. I was home, where I belonged.

Daddy never let me go with him. He put me off from year to year. "If anything happened to you, B.J., I'd never forgive myself," he said. It was much later when I was at summer camp, that I finally got to go on a fishing boat. I did not get seasick, as my father had predicted. I did get a sunburn, not so bad as to leave scars as one did later at Miami Beach, but painful nonetheless. I saw Paul Green's "Common Glory" with a Noxema jar in my hand and knees that felt like heated radiators.

Mamma and I drove over to Williamsburg. Then, you could see everything in one day. These early trips not only instilled in me pride in my native state but engendered a love of history that has carried over into my adult life.

The longest trip Mamma and I took was to visit Uncle Jerome on his fruit ranch in the state of Washington. I was only four years old at the time, so my memories of the trip are spotty. We went by bus and, believe me, buses were not what they are now. They were short and dumpy, with the luggage rack on top. There was no air-conditioning and no toilet. The seat covers were hard bristles that scratched my bare legs.

I do have some memories of that trip, however. The sunset on the Bay and Golden Gate Bridge was breath taking. I remember being afraid I would fall in the Grand Canyon. I remember the size and smell of the redwood trees, and the restaurant inside one of the trees. I also remember holding a piece of petrified wood in my hand from the forest of the same name.

The locust attack in the middle of America was frightening enough not to be forgotten. "There they are," the bus driver called in a high squeaky voice. The sun was beating on the bus so you could believe you were Gretel in the oven. Everyone started closing the windows. Even before the job was done, beads of sweat formed on the upper lip. Outside, the fields shimmered in the heat.

Ahead was a solid black cloud. As we neared no one spoke.

Suddenly the sun disappeared as though swallowed in a black hole. The sounds of thousands of tiny black bodies hurled against the metal sides and windows of the bus was an ancient drum beat of sound. Their whirring was a banshee sound.

Some got in around the windows. Their hard bodies landed like bee stings. Their perpetual motion feet moving a continuous tickle in bare flesh.

And then slowly you began to hear the sound of the bus engine again. Then the wiper blades swooshed locust, left-right and then left again.

As suddenly as it disappeared, the sun shone again. The sigh of relief was almost visible. Windows were flung open. Ladies stood and daintly dusted locust carcasses off the seats. Men fanned with broad brimmed straw hats.

The only thing that had really changed was where there had been broad fields of gold grain on either side of the road as far as the eye could see, now there was nothing but stubble and the insect carcases almost too small to see.

There was also my bad nosebleed on the desert. It was not until I was 12 years old, and the docter burned the vein, too close to the skin, in my nose, that I ever stopped having those nosebleeds that sapped my energy. It was not at all unusual for my parents to have to rush me to the doctor's office in the middle of the night to have my nose cauterized to stop one of those dreadful nosebleeds. Then they would have to carry me home for I was too weak to walk.

I have a very wacky sense of humor. I was sitting in the operating room with the doctor on a stool in front of me. He applied the red hot instrument to the inside of my nose. The hair inside my nose caught fire. I looked like an honest-to-God dragon. The doctor puffed out his cheeks like the north wind and blew out the fire to the accompaniment of gales of my laughter.

I remember going with Uncle Jerome for the cows when the skies were the color of a rusty bucket. We stepped around the cow turds that hid in the shadows and he talked to me like I was a real person and not just a kid.

There were other enjoyable times, too. I sat on the fence beside the orchard in the hot sun. Some workers, "hands," were loading crates, while others loaded those already filled in the truck. I sat watching the operation while eating a freshly pulled apricot. The taste of the fruit and the feel of the warm juice running down my chin was good.

Not so pleasant was the nausea I experienced from the ether I was given so the doctor could remove my thumbnail and get to the soft splinter underneath. All went well until we got on the elevator to leave the building. Some sicknesses we remember with dislike all our lives. That was one of mine.

Much of my childhood was spent in bed recovering from something or other. I had measles, chicken pox, chest colds, nasal drip, and anything else that came my way. I had no resistance to disease. No wonder I'm a vitamin freak.

While we were visiting Uncle Jerome, I was invited to a cousin's birthday party. He was a little hellcat. I don't remember what he looked like but I do remember he had a temper tantrum. He lay on the floor kicking and screaming and finally managed to turn his cake upside down. I watched wide-eyed, expecting God to strike him dead. I didn't know children were allowed to act that way.

On that trip, for the first time in my young life, I heard a language other than English. The small dark woman and her black-eyed child got on the bus somewhere in Texas. The woman wore brightly colored clothes and black nail polish. A steady stream of Mexican Spanish flowed between mother and son. I was charmed and very curious to know what they were saying. I'll never know.

All of our trips were not extensive. Mamma and I quite often packed a lunch and went on short trips after church. My father, of course, did not accompany us. "I did all the traveling I wanted to during World War I," he said. He had come straight out of high school ("Not many people had a chance to go to high school where your father came from," I was told) and joined the Army. He lost hearing in one ear and had pleurisy during the time he was in Europe. He spent time in both France and England. He had seen the world. When he got home he found that the government would pay for him to go to college but not for his books or a place to live, so he went to work at the mill. That is what I mean by a copout on life. If things don't go the way you want them to, don't push.

Mamma and I would drive up the Shenandoah Valley in the spring to see the peach and apple blossoms. In the fall we would go to the James River to see the beautiful colors of the trees. We also visited old churches, and saw Natural Bridge so many times that it became boring. These mini-tours were both fun and educational.

I was so enamored of travel that I went through a stage of wanting to be an airline hostess. That was later, of course.

My only experience with airplanes as a child was one brief Sunday afternoon flight in a Piper Clup. Aunt Lydia had to go with me. "There is no way in this world you'll ever get me in an airplane," Mamma declared. I can say one thing for her, she was true to her word.

My love of being on the road came to an end years later with the crunch of metal on a North Carolina highway on a foggy August morning. I was asleep in Virginia when the accident occurred. Eight people died. I knew four of them. Hearing the sixty-seven year old mother of one victim cry out all night, "Why not me, GOD? Why not me?" chilled my blood.

Walking into a funeral parlor room and seeing four caskets, two adult's and two children's, froze the marrow of my bones. Looking at four bruised and crushed faces that didn't look like anyone I'd talked to last week, took all of the starch out of my spine.

For years, I had nightmares about that experience anytime I knew I had to travel. I finally was able to bed-down the ghosts by writing a poem. In my mind, what happened and the nightmares are inseparable.

My greatest travel pleasure now is to fly. The first commercial flight I made was when the three children and I flew to Ireland. I was the biggest kid of all. I loved it. Just give me a seat belt and a Bloody Mary and I'll go anywhere. For me, flying is addictive, and I'm hooked.

On that trip I also learned that if I can close up the house for six weeks and go from here to another country with an 11-year-old, a 5-year-old and a 3-year-old, there isn't much I can't do.

I'm learning the joy of auto travel all over again. Getting behind the wheel and putting miles between me and here, drawing toward there with every turn of the wheels, is really great.

Mamma hated to ride on a train but, for the sake of my education, we went on a train trip, I loved it. The velvet seats were gritty, but the soot and coal burning smells were unique. My grandfather worked for the railroad. He did not travel but, for years, he spent his days painting engines, those huge black monsters of the rails.

I was a small child on a warm summer, cricket-filled night. I squatted beside the window in my thin summer gown trying to count the stars. The train whistle was far in the distance. It was the most lonesome sound in the world.

I heard the boy coming down the road whistling "Red Wing." He was really good. The sound of the train and the whistling complemented each other. Only the night and one small girl were listening.

Many of my travels were not a physical transference at all. I am a dreamer, and, as Carl Sandburg said, "a hoper." There is nothing so wild that the imagination cannot fill it out like flesh and bones. Someone once said that all deeds begin with an idea in someone's mind. Ideas are but dreams organized.

Being an only child, I spent a lot of my time in my imaginary world. In summer, I lay on my back in the grass, making pictures out of cloud formations. I lay on my belly, watching ants go seriously about their lives. I lay on my bed dreaming I would grow up pretty. It was many years before I could accept myself as not being right-down-ugly. That was a great relief. As a child I was told, "Why don't you be yourself?" when I tried to conform to my peers; "Why don't you be like everybody else?" when I deviated. It messes up your self-image when you are trying so hard to please.

I escaped to my dreams. There I could be anything or nothing, as I pleased. I was a famous movie star. I was Scarlett O'Hara, with better discrimination; I'd never let Rhett go. I was the heroine being put upon by men or refusing to let such a thing happen. I was Wonder Woman and Little Neil. I could be anybody and do anything without devoting my whole life in dedication to service.

Dreams are how you pluck stars from the sky. They are also what feed the writer with materials which are sorted logically into patterns you will accept and believe. Yes, I am a dreamer who has found a way to channel my imaginings into your mind, too.

Chapter 9

Changes

The things that happen in a child's life could change that life or even end it. "God watches over drunks and children," old women say with a cluck of the tongue. I believe this each time I see my son swing from the top of a tree and then get safely on the ground.

On that bitter cold afternoon when I was playing in the snow, scooping up hands-full of cold with wet mittens, I could all but taste the white of the icy moisture that melted on chattering teeth and slid without effort down my throat.

"Come on," my friends called from the road. They did not wear clumsy galoshes, like me, but wrapped chains around their feet forming cleats that scarred the snow.

Of all the things I hated as a child, galoshes were high on the list. They were hard to get on, looked ugly, and made my feet sweat. Besides, I always associated galoshes with old women who no longer cared what they looked like or maybe never did. "Give me comfort every time," they defended.

That afternoon I stood squinting in the bright, cold sunshine. The light on the snow made it look like so many diamonds begging to be picked up. On the other hand, maybe each snowflake was trying to detach itself from the others: "Look at me. Look at me. I am so beautifully unique, I don't need the others. See how I reflect the light."

"Where are you going?" I called to my friends.

"There's been a bus wreck," they answered, not stopping for small talk.

A bus wreck, wow! We had never had that much excitement in our community in all my memory. My heart beat faster. My breath fogged like cigarette smoke in the movies or the balloons over comic-strip characters. "Anybody hurt?" I asked into my balloon of breath.

"Yeah," they called walking faster. "There's blood and everything."

I walked along the edge of the yard, trying to follow them. In my excitement and desire not to miss out on the fun, I all but jumped up and down. "How far?" I asked.

"Not far," they called and gave me a look I understood well. It was accusing. 'Mamma's baby can't go out of the yard.' 'See the little girl play in the snow.' The words were as plainly seen in their look as the words "See Spot run" were in my reading book.

"You coming or not, B.J.? We ain't got all day," one called.

"She better not," another said.

"She'll get a lickin' sure as shooting."

I glanced toward the house. It was as white as the snow with its green roof fringed with icicles. Smoke puffed from the kitchen chimney. There would be soup for supper. It might be vegetable soup with lots of tomatoes served with hunks of cornbread or maybe potato soup with huge chunks of potatoes and onions.

My heart beat faster. It wasn't fair. It just wasn't fair to have to stay in my own yard when there was something so exciting just over the ridge. I looked from the house to my friends and back again.

"Well," one of them called. "What are you going to do?"

I could feel tears ready to come but I blinked them back. It was being a baby to cry. I wanted to go with them and yet I knew that if I asked permission I would not get to go. I began to tremble but not from the cold. I hoped my friends could not see me shake as I crossed the ditch and joined them on the roadside. I just had to go. No retelling of the events of the afternoon could ever replace seeing for myself. "Blood," they had said.

41

Was the bus turned over or just leaning at an angle? Was anyone hurt badly? Why someone might be dying this very minute with great gasps of pain, and we were missing it.

"Ain't you going to tell your mamma?" one asked.

I dared not speak for fear of revealing my fear. I shook my head and set my gaze straight ahead and did not look back.

"Good old B.J.," one boy said, giving me such a clump between my shoulder blades that I almost went face first in a snow drift. "Sometimes I think you're chicken, but I reckon you ain't so bad."

It was a good mile to where the bus lay on its side with luggage and people scattered about. People stood around in quiet tight clusters just as they did between Sunday School and preaching.

We knew that children were to be seen and not heard. We also knew that if we just stood around and listened, we would find out what happened.

"I didn't even see that patch of ice," the hatless driver told the old man beside him. "I swear I never saw it." He was pale and obviously shaken by the experience.

I knew the farmer he was talking to. He was an old man with a drooping mustache and a rusty old felt hat. On Friday afternoons he delivered buttermilk and eggs to our house. It was thick, rich buttermilk with flecks of butterfat floating in it. The eggs were big and brown.

The old man would sit at our kitchen table red-faced. His breath came in great wheezing gulps. Mamma told me that, in ragweed time, he had to sleep sitting in a chair beside the cold pot-bellied stove because his asthma was so bad.

Sometimes, when the old man was sick, we would go to his house to pick up the milk and eggs. I can still remember the sweet smell of warm milk that permeated the air in that house and I remember seeing the oil cloth covered table in the kitchen that was always set for the next meal or the next hungry visitor. I remember eating biscuits still warm from supper topped with hunks of butter and drowned in honey the color of amber and the taste of ambrosia.

When the sun went behind a cloud on the afternoon of the wreck, I shivered. It would be best if I got out of sight before the egg man noticed me and started to ask questions I did not want to answer.

I slipped around the corner of the house only to learn that my friends had gotten bored even before I had. They were eyeing a small icy pond.

"It sure would be fun," one said.

"What?" I asked, not wanting to miss any of the fun.

"We were just talking about going skating."

I looked at the pond. I knew all about Hans Brinker and the silver skates but that was in Holland and we were in Virginia.

"Yep, it sure would be fun," one friend said, stuffing his cold reddened fists in his pockets.

"You couldn't go skating with those chains on your feet," I said. We seldom had enough snow for a good sleigh ride, much less enough ice to skate on.

My friend looked down at his feet.

"They come off real easy. I could take them off." That answer satisfied me. It made perfectly good sense.

"Yeah, but who's going to test the ice?" my other friend asked.

I looked from one of them to the other. They were both looking at me. I frowned and looked at the pond again. It didn't look very large or deep and it certainly seemed iced in solid. I shook my head. "I can't swim."

"You ain't going to swim. You're going to skate."

"Yeah, B.J. You'll be the first one in the whole county to go ice skating in years."

"Besides, we'll hold on to you, B.J., old buddy, old pal."

"Ain't nobody can say our friend B.J.'s afraid of nothing."

I was still looking at the pond. It sure looked safe enough. All of my friends would be jealous if they knew I was braver than my friends and was the first one to set foot on the ice. It did not occur to me that I might also become the first drowning victim in years.

"Come on, B.J., you can do it."

I walked closer to the pond. What had happened to the goldfish I had seen there last summer? Had their sleek and shiny bodies shrunk to the size of ice cubes that were being stored in the muddy pond floor waiting for spring thaws and bird calls to help pump life back into their bodies? Maybe they had been fished out with small nets, like guppies in the dime store, and were now safely swimming around and around a glass aquarium inside the warm house.

"Come on, B.J. Don't take all day."

A cold breeze got under my ear flaps and whistled around my ears. "Hold onto my sleeve," I said.

One boy caught my sleeve as I put one foot on the ice. The other caught my coat tail. I put my weight on the foot on the ice. I could feel how slippery the surface was even with my rubber galoshes. "I don't think this is going to work," I said.

"Sure it is ," one friend said, "See, the ice never cracked or nothing. Why it's as solid as a rock bed."

We all understood about rock beds. For the past summer and fall, we had spent a lot of time watching the construction of a new road through our valley.

"Now, don't get too close to the workers, B.J.," I was told. "They're prisoners."

"What kind of prisoners?" I asked.

"They're men who've done bad things. Some of them have murdered people and some of them have stolen money."

I studied the prisoners very closely that summer. I studied the shapes of their faces and the look in their eyes. Some of them frightened me but most shared a common expression — despair. I felt pity for those men and yet in my young mind I reasoned that if they had done something terrible then they had to pay the price for their deeds even as I had to pay for misconduct. Yet, I felt there must be a better way to pay than spend long days with a pick and shovel under the watchful eyes of a guard with a shotgun across his knees. The world's problems were just too great for one small girl to solve in a single hot summer.

"Go on, B.J.," my friend urged. "Put your other foot on the ice and then we'll join you." I did, but exactly what happened next, I am not sure. They tell me the ice seemed to all crack at once. They also tell me that it sounded like the blast from a shotgun. All I remember was a sudden numbing cold like I had never known before. The next thing I remember was sitting by a red hot pot-bellied stove wrapped in a blanket. "We've called your father, B.J. He's coming to get you." My teeth were chattering too much for me to speak.

Someone handed me a steaming cup of hot tea which I took between trembling fingers. I remember how the tea burned its way down my throat and into my stomach. Its warmth seemed to spread through my whole body.

When I calmed down enough to look around, I learned that some of the bus passengers had been hurt. Beside the lace-covered front window, a man sat on a couch. One arm was held in place by a makeshift sling fashioned from an old sheet, still white but worn. In his other hand the man held the stub of a cigarette. He sat looking at the floor as though he could tell from the worn feather-patterned linoleum where he was and why he should be there.

Near me in an old rocker sat a woman with a bandage around her head. She sat with her head leaned back and her eyes closed. The color of her face was that of cold ashes on a mountain hearth on an early morning. Her lips moved as she fingered the prayer beads held so lovingly between her arthritis-gnarled fingers. I studied her face trying to determine where a woman like that would be going on a bus in the middle of the winter. It seemed to me she should be at home knitting ear warmers for her sons and warm scarves for her grandchildren. I felt sorry for her. It must be a very important mission to bring her out in such weather.

"Do you want more tea?" the lady of the house asked.

I felt very guilty because I had been caught staring at the woman near me. I not only knew that it was rude to stare, but I knew why.

The fall before, I had gone for a walk in the woods near my home. By the time I got home my face was burning and itching. It was not long before my face began to swell. Mother called the doctor and yes he would see me.

The big problem was transportation. My father had driven our only car to work. I had to ride the bus. People stared at me through car windows as I stood on the side of the road waiting for the bus. One woman on the bus grabbed her child, "Stay away from her, child. It's no telling what she's got." By the time I got to the doctor's office I was completely cowed. It was then I swore I would never stare at anyone. We cause each other enough pain without meaning to, much less adding more conflict to an already burdened spirit.

But I had been caught staring at that woman even if she didn't know I was looking. "No, ma'am," I replied humbly. "I won't have more tea."

It seemed a very long time before my father came. The two injured people had been taken to a hospital. Most of the curious who had come to see had left. My friends I learned later, had only stayed around long enough to be sure the passing truck driver had fished me out of the pond alive. The lady of the house was stuffing chunks of wood in the cookstove while singing snatches of "Abide With Me." I sat huddled in the chair waiting for the knock I knew would come and dreading what my father would say and do.

I had time enough to worry many ideas around in my head. I was too tired to consider running away from home. If I got spanked, I just would. All I could really concentrate on was praying for the strength to get through whatever ordeal that faced me (people in the Bible always did that) and thinking about how warm and good it would be to be home in bed with a towel-wrapped hot water bottle at my feet. "God, if you grant me this one wish, I won't ask for anything else for a very long time. I won't even ask for a new doll at Christmas but I'll take good care of the ones I have."

My stomach growled. "And, God, I sure would like a bowl of hot soup."

The rap on the door was not loud, but I jumped before pulling the blanket around me. It was near dusk and I could not see the expression in his face. "I brought her fresh clothes," he said to the lady of the house.

"Her others are wet through and through," she replied. They were steaming over the fire with the smell of wet wool.

Daddy's voice sounded calm enough, but maybe he was just being a nice grownup person. I had to ride the mile home with him in the car — alone. I quickly put on the clothes he brought and added my thanks to Daddy's for her hospitality.

When we got in the car, he said, "You all right, B.J.?"

"Yes, sir," I mumbled being grateful for the familiarity of place.

46

He started the car and shifted into gear before speaking. "You sure gave us a scare."

"I did?" I asked. Instead of being angry he was concerned. He really cared about me.

"Yes, you did. We love you very much and want you to grow up to be a fine woman and not die from some Tom-fool kid stunt." He paused and looked at me out of the corner of his eye. "It's a wonder any kid ever grows up, B.J." He chuckled. "When you get old enough and have children of your own, I'll tell you about some of the things my brother and I did as kids."

I sneaked across the seat and tucked my head under his arm. "I'm so glad to be back," I said, already half asleep.

"We're glad to have you back, too, baby," he said.

No words ever rang more beautifully in my ears. "Papa," I said. It was a term of endearment that I only used in our most personal conversations. The only problem was, I forgot what I was going to say. I was warm, happy, going home and almost asleep. The feeling of being close and being loved even made the dousing worthwhile.

I learned that being alive is worth more than being first at anything. I also learned that those who challenged me stood far back in the wings. They dared nothing and gained nothing. I found out that you have to take a chance, if you expect to gain anything

Chapter 10

Then Was The Music

You do not stay a little kid all of your life, no matter how long it seems. Your shoes get too small and you outgrow your dresses. Slowly you get a figure. For some of us that takes longer than others.

The report cards stack up in the family file. The fifth-grade report is under the sixth, and you are in junior high and then high school.

Then, all of the grades were in one building but you moved to different parts of the building. We carried larger and larger stacks of books.

We were not very democratic about who we associated with. Our families went back for generations and we all knew, or thought we did, who was acceptable and who was not. The fact that none of us had a lot of money made the foundation of good family even more important. "But, we don't know anything about them," was a phase often used to discourage a school friendship that might not be accepted at home.

I will never forget the time Ida Faye Long came home with me from school. She was a nice girl with the all-arms-and-legs shape of the rest of us. Her clothes were homemade, but she was always immaculately clean. She came to school with her face shining from the scrub of a cloth and her hair still damp from washing. "Howdy do, ma'am," she said to Mamma.

"And whose child are you?" Mamma asked, as she put the grocery store premium dishes on the table. (That is a characteristic that still carries over into my life. I search out premiums. If the everyday dishes are chipped and you can get some at a bargain price at the grocery check-out counter, do it.)

"I'm Johnny and Sue Ellen Long's," Ida Faye said.

"You seem like a nice child," Mamma said, as she ladeled beans into a bowl.

Ida Faye did not catch what Mamma said, but I did. Mamma said "seem." That meant that she was on probation. "Seem" meant maybe yes and maybe no. In other words, "We'll see."

I prayed for Ida Faye. "Dear God, don't let her make a mistake." If she did, our friendship was over.

Mamma did not usually openly disapprove of my friends. She did make them sound less and less desirable — not only as friends but as people.

When we sat at the table, Ida Faye looked from one of us to the other expectantly. The odor of pork chops, beans, macaroni, and cornbread had my mouth watering.

We bowed our heads for the blessing. I looked out of the corner of my eyes and saw a puzzled look on Ida Faye's face. I punched her with my elbow and motioned for her to do what we were.

"All right, B.J.," Mamma said.

"God is good. God is great," I said by rote. My children learned the same blessing. They used to say they could tell how hungry I was by how fast I said the blessing.

All was going as usual until the macaroni was passed to Ida Faye. She looked at the bowl and then looked at me.

It was my favorite dish. "Have some," I said. I wanted to help her, but I could feel Mamma's look.

"Don't mind if I do," she said.

The moment of panic was over, or so I thought. The next day at school, between classes, Ida Faye asked, "What was that stuff that was so good?"

When I got home, Mamma asked, "Where does that child come from who has never seen macaroni?" Mamma had a way of knowing things.

One thing that Mamma knew was that music gave her a headache. Outside of "Rock of Ages," she did not care for music. She was particularly unimpressed by what she referred to as "That caterwalling in a foreign tongue that nobody can understand but a heathen."

Although my friend Jerry would eventually major in music in college and then go on to write his own musicals and own his own music company, he was just learning then. I was his most avid fan, and I fell madly in love with Rachmaninoff.

"Play it again, Jerry," I said.

"I've already played it three times," he said, as he slouched on the piano stool with his lower lip stuck out.

"But it's so beautiful," I pleaded. "Just one more time. You only made one mistake last time."

He glanced at me with a look that could cut my throat. "I did not make a mistake." There were icicles in his words.

I ignored his warning signals. "Please, just once more."

"I don't want to," he said, getting up from the piano stool.

"You're mean," I said, as I stuck out my lower lip. "You're acting spoiled," that is what Mamma always said to me. "You're doing just what you want to."

"Go home, B.J." He stood with his fists on his hips. "Go home right now."

"Not until you play again," I said stubbornly.

"Yes, you will," he said, as he reached for the broom his mother had left leaning against the piano. "You go home or I'll hit you."

One look at his flushed face and the angry glint in his dark eyes made a believer out of me. "Someday when I'm rich and famous, you'll be sorry you treated me this way," I said, as I went out the door.

He had the broom raised over his head and looked as though he might pursue me. "And don't ever come back."

"Don't worry, I won't," I called over my shoulder, as I jumped over the pansy bed and ran for the front gate. When Jerry got that angry, you got out of his way. He didn't have red hair for nothing.

By the next day we had forgiven, if not forgotten, our disagreement. It is a good thing, too, since there were many such spats. We argued with fervor.

It was not until later, however, when The Philadelphia Philharmonic Orchestra gave a performance at the Opera

House in the city near us that I saw a live performance by professional musicians. It was a matinee, and we went on school buses. Even now, it delights me to see my children on their way to a concert or ballet because I remember the pleasures of that rainy afternoon long ago.

The large auditorium was filled with chattering young people and excited teachers. Just because we did not live in a major city did not mean we lacked the desire for the arts or the ability to appreciate them.

A hush fell over the auditorium as the lights dimmed. There was an electricity in the silence that all the previous noise had not had. Even those of us who did not know what to expect when the curtain rose waited with baited breath.

All eyes were focused on those curtains. Slowly they began to rise. I gasped. Literally every inch of the stage was occupied with musicians and instruments. How in the world could all of those people possibly hope to play the same music at the same time?

One man stood alone crisply alert in his tuxedo and starched collar. He bowed toward us, then turned and raised his baton.

Then was the music. The beautiful music. It filled your ears and sank into your soul. I didn't even try to wipe the tears. Beauty is not just seen with the eyes. It is heard with the ears. It creeps in through the skin and is stored in the mind.

After the performance, when I was home again and watching the rain running like tears down my window pane, I sat with my hands folded in my lap and thought about what I had experienced.

I saw a squirrel under the oak tree gathering nuts and nervously chattering. I saw a robin in the dogwood tree and heard him sing the glad news of being alive. The cat rubbed a soft side and purred his content, and it was then I knew that the whole world is filled with music, if we will just listen to it. Even silence has its own harmony.

Chapter 11

One Smart Day

It was June fifth in the Year of Our Lord and the day I graduated from high school at the ripe old age of 16. I was smarter that day than I ever was before or have been since. Everybody needs one smart day in a lifetime. That was mine.

Ahead of me, I could see life opening like a flower. I could sense that my future would be different from my past. About that, at least I was correct. The summer months ahead of me were the buffer zone between me and an entirely different way of life. I had already been accepted at Corinth College.

What I didn't know was that learning is never done. There is no such thing as being educated, for to stop learning is to die. Who knows? Death, too, may just be another step in the development of the soul. Since I haven't been there yet, I neither know nor am anxious to learn.

The main development of that June day was my receiving the diploma that legally declared that the school had done all it could for me, and from that date I was somebody else's problem. I am not sure my blue and white pumps even touched the floor.

"Well, B.J.," the principal said, holding my diploma just out of reach. "I could tell a lot of stories about you." He paused and gave me a crooked grin. He could tell some things. If he did, I knew a hole would open in the floor and swallow me. "But I won't," he said. I began to breathe again.

I studied my reflection in the mirror. Yes, I was a big girl now. I wore lipstick, earrings, high-heeled shoes and a bra, although there was little need for one. I liked the sparkle in my eyes. I was happy, if not too bright. Then I didn't know I was really Peter Pan and would never grow up.

Chapter 12

The War

My only reason for being a child was so that I could grow into something better. Being a child was a bore, and all of the adults were telling me it was the best time of my life. "You better enjoy being a kid," my uncle. "You'll be an adult a long time," God have mercy on those who only can look back on childhood. I remember too many long afternoons with nothing to do but talk to the cat or watch the squirrels bury nuts.

I was an observer from the sidelines of life lived more intensely than at other times. It was World Was II. All service men were handsome and all young women were beautiful. There were meetings and partings of such intensity that it is difficult, if not impossible, to understand in times of peace. But the war went on and on, eating such a chunk out of my life that I really could remember nothing else. War was — is — and ever shalt be. How could anyone be so crass as to think of the future when our boys were being killed both singly and in numbers? We heard about it over the radio from such men as Lowell Thomas, Edward R. Murrow and H.B. Kaltenborn. When the news was on, all of America listened and woe be unto a child who made any noise. We saw what was happening on the silver screen in the RKO & PATHE newsreels. There were pictures of ships with the decks covered with our boys, their heads bandaged or legs gone.

Since I was too young to kiss the boys goodbye, I responded with rabid patriotism. I loathed the enemy and loved our brave men with fervor. I collected grease, jumped up and down on tin cans, wore homemade underwear, and sold war bonds.

My friend, Jerry, and I went out in our boots and coats with homemade scarves around our necks. Our breath puffed Lucky Strike smoke rings. The ground crunched under our feet in the late winter afternoon light. We knew we were not as cold as our troops in Europe. We had boots, didn't we? Maybe they didn't. We had warm scarves, and maybe they didn't even have enough clothes.

"You reckon Mrs. Davis will buy one?" Jerry asked.

I knew a part of what I felt was excitement and not just cold. "I don't know; I hear she's pretty tight with a buck."

"Wonder where she gets money from anyway? She's old and alone." He kicked a gravel out of the road.

We came nearer her house and I was feeling really spooked. I did not know the woman, but I had seen her with a scarf over her head, out in her yard gathering wood. It was the combination of her pointed chin, long nose, and the scarf, I'm sure, but I felt certain she was a witch. Her small house reminded me of Hansel and Gretel, the story I would not let my father finish reading when I was quite small sitting on the edge of his bed in the pool of light from the lamp that hung on the head of the bed in the dark room. I could not bear for those brave children to be pushed into the oven like pullets to be roasted. Was it our turn?

"Do come in, children," she said. Her voice was dry as an old leaf that cracked in your hand when you touched it. "Come in out of the cold. If not for your sakes, for mine. The cold is hard on my bones." She shuffled on the worn cold linoleum floor in Grant's felt houseshoes with rubber bands holding them on. "Selling bonds, you say? I'll have to see."

Jerry and I stood in the middle of her tiny parlor looking around. Our breath fogged in front of us, for there was no heat in the room. The furnishings were sparse and shabby. She had certainly accumulated very little to be as old as she was. I was already oriented to value possessions.

"It sure is cold in here," Jerry said.

My teeth were chattering. There was a musty smell in the room and something else that I did not recognize then as the odor of decaying flesh.

55

The old woman did not have the money to buy a bond, so we bundled up inside our mittens and ear muffs and went out into the cold dusk. It was one of those eerie evenings when the sun is not visible. The sky was the pink-purple of a science fiction story. The snow looked dingy with deep shadows where footsteps had broken the surface. Our footfalls crunched as we trudged beside the railroad tracks. I thought I heard something move. "Did you hear that?"

"No," Jerry said, walking faster. One look at his face made me think he did. We both knew that a hobo had tried to hop a freight just about where we were and missed. I walked faster, too.

One thing bothered me when I heard about the hobo. "He's just an old bum. Nobody's going to miss him," someone said. How could anyone die and have no one to grieve? It wasn't natural in the world I lived in. You were supposed to have a casket, flowers, and lots of people crying. Well, if no one else cared, I did. I held the first of my childhood religious services. I sang hymns, prayed for his immortal soul, and grieved. After all, I had to do it all myself. It was very serious and sad.

Knowing I had done all I could for the nameless man did not give me confidence as I hurried along to keep up with Jerry. It seemed there was a presence going step for step. I looked around very carefully. I saw nothing. If you can't see something, it isn't there, right? Or is it?

We did more than sell bonds, we collected grease and tin cans. Recycling is not something new. We also counted very carefully the gas and food rationing stamps. Daddy even made his own cigarettes. I still remember the contraption he used. It was shaped like a mule. You put the tobacco and paper in the mule's mouth. The completed cigarette came out the other end. It was really something to watch, and I felt quite naughty just observing. Being a patriot called for a lot of sacrifices, as well as overt efforts.

Underwear material was scarce, if not unavailable. I will never forget the magic words, "parachute silk." It not only felt good against the skin, it made you feel good that one of Our Boys was not going to spill his guts on a foreign field because his parachute didn't open.

Mamma drove miles for other forms of underwear and sleep-wear material. I'll never forget my pink satin underpants. They were a real shock to my bed-warmed bottom on cold and unheated, bedroom mornings. For some reason, I always drew pink as the proper color for drawers. I will never forget one pair. They were beautifully sewn soft pink — with rosebuds, for goodness sake.

On my way home from school, the elastic broke in the waist of these beauties. My snowpants kept them from falling around my ankles, but they fell around my knees. If I had a sense of humor, I would have laughed. I tried to walk with dignity. After all, I was a noble Virginian.

"You want to write to my brother?" Misty asked.

I was sitting on the side of the bed, putting red-red lipstick on my lips. I was not allowed to wear lipstick, of course, but this was an old tube that belonged to Misty's sister, who was 18. You had to concentrate, or one slip of the tube and you looked like a Sunday-morning comic that had been rained on.

"He'll write to anybody," she said. I did not know her brother but I had seen his picture. He was a cute little sailor with dark curly hair and lots of teeth in his smile.

I blotted the lipstick on a tissue and picked up the make-believe cigarette (a rolled piece of paper) and blew imaginary smoke in the air. Lauren Bacall had nothing on me. "No thanks," I drawled. "I've got all I can do to write my cousins."

"Cousins are relatives," she said with a sneer. "They don't count."

I was not deceived. If it was her brother, that was one thing. My cousins were the brothers I didn't have. Boy, was I proud of them. Two were in the Air Force, one was in the Army, and one was in the Navy. She had only one brother. "I wouldn't know what to say," I shrugged.

She bent over, intent on fastening the ankle strap of her big sister's shoe. Legs look better when mounted on high heels. "Tell him you love him. You don't have to mean it. That's what all the girls say."

I began to sweat (Mamma would say "perspire"). I loved playing grown-up, but that didn't mean I wanted to be one. "What if Mamma found out?"

"Rent a Post Office box," she suggested, as she wobbled across the floor. "It is mysterious," she said balancing herself with outstretched arms.

"It's crazy," I said with a giggle. I only wrote my cousins. Her brother would have to find his own true love. I wasn't the one.

We kids could not be brave and sacrificing all of the time, so we sought escape.

We went to the movies.

I bled with red-haired Mrs. Miniver and kissed every boy with Jennifer Jones. It did not matter that they were but shadows on the wall. They were more real to me than the world I lived in. I really wanted to believe.

I would go to see anything with Cornell Wilde or Errol Flynn. I loved those swashbuckling feats of chandelier swinging and pirate ship boardings. They always got the girl, and I sat there imagining each beautiful woman was me. I really believed the ugly duckling story. I did not confine my love of adventure to the movies. I read every book I could get my hands on. It did not seem strange to me that, no matter what horrible things the characters went through, they were just as beautiful at the end of the story as at the beginning.

My taste in movies ranged from one extreme to the other. All that mattered was what happened to be on when I had the time and money to go. It would be difficult to count the times I saw such things as "Gone With The Wind," "The Wizard of Oz," or "The Trail of The Lonesome Pine." I saw all of the composers' and artists' lives. Oh, how they suffered for Art. I roamed with Lassie, and spent Sunday afternoon South of the Border with Gene Autry and his horse.

Of course, high on the list were the war movies. John Wayne and Alan Ladd were heroes not to be ignored. I really believed that John Wayne carried a machine gun on his hip, and I was right there to help him kill, kill, kill and make all right with the world. I hated all over the place.

Not only did I do battle both in Europe and the Pacific, but I danced with all of the hoofers who dazzled the eyes of a romantic child. Just because she was beautiful, gave Mitzi Gaynor no right to ignore that loveable sailor, Gene Kelly. I knew all along that they would "find each other." How could they resist? Theirs was not a romance made in heaven but on the back lot of the movie studio.

Meanwhile, my learning to deal with people developed very slowly, if at all. Whether it was because I lived so much in a dream world, or because I was really afraid of people, I will never know, but I did not relate well with my peers. In fact, it was not until I got into college that I really made friends.

As a child, I was a loner. Partly this was my own fault, for friendship was something I learned to avoid. I would confide to some girl that I liked a certain boy and she would immediately tell the boy. I would go around for a week red-faced.

I filled volumes of diaries. Years later, I looked back at them and wanted to cry. If only I hadn't taken everything so seriously.

One friend betrayed me less often than others. Eleanor was our neighbor. She was tall, blonde and quite pretty. She had moved there with her husband and their small daughter. She was my confidant, but even she went to my mother from time to time with tidbits I had imparted in secrecy. These came back to me in the form of: "What is a little girl like you talking about boys for?" or, "Why are you telling everybody—?" In fact I was not telling everybody, so I knew where the information came from. What an evil person I saw myself to be for the things that were going through my mind. Surely other girls didn't worry the way I did. Mamma should have encouraged me to become a nun. That would have been one salvation for a soul as black and depraved as mine.

Despite all my misgivings I did date one boy during high school. His grandfather had dated my grandmother, and so my family approved of him immensely. All I saw in him was transportation to parties and ball games. I was not crass; just honest. He was a farmer and a very good one. He was always immaculately clean. His complexion was ruddy and he was short and overweight. "You can't go off to college," he told me.

I not only could, but would. I had lived the first 16 years of my life for this chance, and I was not about to miss my opportunity. I wanted to meet people who could carry on a decent conversation. They were out there in the big wide world, and I was going to find them. I wanted to meet new boys, from someplace other than my own valley. You bet your sweet life I was going, and I had no intention of ever coming home for any length of time.

Even in the dark car, I could tell he was crying. I found the whole situation very embarrassing. I should have felt something more, but I didn't. "I'm going," I heard myself say.

"You'll come back. You'll come back before Christmas and marry me."

The very idea horrified me. I had no intention of marrying anyone for a very long time, and there was no way I was going to be a farm wife. I had seen too many of them grow old under the burden of too much hard work. I had other plans for my life. "I'm going," I said. "Now take me home."

He tried to put his arms around me. I pushed him away. "Take me home right now."

"But, honey."

"Don't honey me, and get your hands off me."

There were no words between us on the way to where I lived. When the car stopped, I opened the door. "Listen, Curt," I said. I could hear the anger in my own voice. "Don't walk me to the door. Don't call me and don't come to see me."

I could see the hurt look on his face that was lit by the dash lights. "You don't mean that."

"Yes, I do, and I won't change my mind." I slammed the door and walked away from him. My hands shook as I opened the door, but I never regretted my decision. It taught me that if I am forced to make a choice I can and it is the right one for me. Decide and don't look back.

World War II and those years after were the ones in which I grew from a child to a young woman. There were some exciting times and some dull, but they were the ones I had.

Chapter 13

At College

The campus of Corinth College was lush with the late fall blossoms still full, with no hint of the cold Kentucky winter that lay ahead. Having come from a very small Virginia high school where the faces you saw every day were the same ones you had seen since first grade, I was impressed with all of the people I saw before we even got to the dormatory. They were all young, like me, with hope shining in their eyes. Corinth was a working college, so none of us had much money. What we did have was the glimpse of a future much brighter than anything in our backgrounds. We were young, and we believed that speaker last June who had told us that the world was our oyster. He had not said how we were to go about diving for it nor how to open it once it was in our hot little hands. Undaunted, we all knew that the world was going to be a better place for having us in it.

When I first got to the dorm room, my roommate's possessions were there but she was not. The room was just large enough for our two beds, wooden desks and chairs, and had not even the slightest resemblance to the pictures of college rooms I had seen in the yearbooks of Virginia schools I had pored over. It was then I had my first doubts. Maybe this was all a mistake. Maybe I didn't belong, and what was my mysterious roommate like? There wasn't much you could tell from a few suitcases and some plastic clothes bags.

61

My things were duly brought into the room and stacked on the side not already occupied. Space was filled, but there was no sense of order or hominess.

A local minister had Mamma and me paged. "Don't worry about a thing, little Mamma," he told her with a protective arm around my shoulder. "I'll take good care of your little girl," he assured her. I never saw him again. My Sunday mornings were spent peacefully in sleep or propped snugly in my bed with a good book. Mamma went home with the warm feeling that her only child was being watched over by one of God's own, and I was left to my own devices. Everybody was happy.

When we got back to the room, it was populated by two blonde-haired children, one mother type, and a tall blonde with an excellent figure. "Hi," the blonde said over her shoulder. She was busy putting her clothes on hangers. "I'm your roommate," she said. "I'm Peaches."

I must have looked at her incredulously, for she laughed and added, "Peaches isn't my real name, of course." She wrinkled her nose. "My real name is Maxine, but I ask you do I look like a 'Maxine' to you?"

It was my turn to smile. "No, but you don't look like a Peaches, either. That sounds like the name of a stripper."

"B.J.," Mamma said over my shoulder, scandalized.

I liked this new roommate of mine, and we built a real friendship that lasted a long time until distance and lifestyles put the kiss of silence on it. Then we talked and planned our futures. How wise we were, lying there in the dark with our wool blankets pulled up under our chins. We swapped clothes so often that not even our best friends knew who belonged to what. We double dated and sometimes vied for the attention of the same young man. This did not happen often, since the ones that were attracted to her were only good friends of mine and the same worked out in the opposite direction. We were Rose Red and Rose White.

The girls who lived on our floor of the dorm were like one big family. We would gather in one room or the other and solve the problems of our world from the time the doors were locked — whether to keep us in or the boys out was never quite clear — until the wee hours of the morning. We were a varied, but not a motley, crew. The oldest was about 24 and had been on her own since she was 15. There were those of us who were still wet behind the ears. The girls came from all kinds of backgrounds. One girl sat wearing nothing but panties, and one went in the closet to put on her pajamas. We talked about home and classes and boys. We patted each others egos, cried together and talked about boys. We shared "care" packages from home and then we talked about boys.

We discussed who was really serious about whom and therefore off limits. What had happened in what class and which teacher was best at what subject. Advice to the lovelorn was everywhere. Most of us had a new crush at least once a week, if not more often.

"Who is that?" I asked Peaches, nodding toward a guy who had just come into the dining room. He was tall with blonde curly hair and very blue eyes.

"I don't know," she said, putting another fork full of food in her mouth. I thought she knew all the boys. We all attacked each meal as though we were starved. The food was not all that good and the word had already spread that, "They put salt peter in the food."

"What's that?"

"Something to keep down our sex drives."

Peaches flipped a blonde curl over her shoulder and said, "His cousin lives across the hall from us. Why don't you go over and introduce yourself? Just tell him you are a friend of his cousin's."

"No," I said, pushing my tray away. "This one is something special. I want a proper introduction."

I started to make friends with his cousin as a cold, calculated plan to get an introduction to the blonde young man who completely ignored me. It was as though I did not exist. The more I got to know the girl across the hall, Mindy, the better I liked her. She represented all the gentle things in life. She even looked gentle, with brown hair and eyes. Her voice was low with a musical laugh to highlight our conversations. I should have been ashamed of my original motive, but I was not. I liked my new friend very much and she is still one of my favorite people.

"Zack?" she questioned, when I finally mentioned that I heard she had a cousin who was also in our class. "You wouldn't like him at all. He isn't your type."

"I'd like to meet him, anyway," I said. "If he's your cousin, he can't be all bad."

She thought a minute. There was a twinkle in her dark eyes. I didn't know then that that was her matchmaker twinkle. "He's all right," she said. "But I just can't see you two together."

"Why?" I asked.

"With his temper and yours, you couldn't possibly get along. Besides, you're an only child and he's the youngest of five. You're both used to having your own way."

"So?"

She pursed her lips. "What sign are you?"

"Sagittarius."

"Well, there you are," she said.

"What is that supposed to mean?"

"He's an Aries. You're both fire signs. You might have an interesting relationship but never a good one."

"Hogwash," I declared.

She introduced us. He said, "Hi," and turned his attention to another girl.

"See," Mindy said. "I told you." She paused, but not for long. "I have another cousin I think you would like better."

I rasied one eyebrow but said nothing. I did not give up that easily. I made a point of being in the dining hall when he was. I sat at a nearby table with my friends. I made it seem that all of the action was at our table.

My dates and I managed to sit, accidently of course, one or two rows in front of Zack and his date at movies and ballgames. It was comforting to notice that he continually dated different girls.

Mindy, my friend and ally, made sure I was invited on all outings that she and Zack were. Two can play the "ignore you" game. I talked to everyone else in the group. When he talked, I wouldn't even look at him.

If we met accidentally, I blushed and rushed on. Inside, I was miserable. My "I'll marry-him-if-I-can" letter had been mailed.

64

"I don't understand why he doesn't ask you out," Mindy said on one bleak evening.

"He will," I replied, not being sure at all.

"You don't know him like I do, B.J. He's stubborn."

"So am I." Did you ever whistle in the dark to keep your courage up?

"I don't know," she said, shaking her head. "Maybe it just isn't meant to be."

"You and that fate business again."

I was close to tears. What I had been studying and what I had been learning had me surrounded by questions marks. The rhetorical who am I? What am I doing? Where am I going? How long will it take me to get there? I was in the middle of a peer society without a concrete authority figure to do battle or comfort. I was in the middle of the best and worst of possible worlds. The complication of Zack I did not need.

"I wish I hadn't introduced you two."

"Nonsense," I said, turning to leave. I gave her a malicious grin. "Anybody could have made that mistake and, besides, I insisted on it."

She chuckled. "Show's what you know."

"Right," I agreed.

"I want you to meet my other cousin."

"Mindy," I said, turning serious. "If it's all the same to you, with the exception of you, I think I'll just leave your family alone."

Not all of my relationships seemed so disastrous. In addition to the girls who lived in the dorm, I made friends with classmates and those I worked with. I had been assigned to wait tables in the college-owned hotel. It was not a bad job and besides, you were allowed to eat such leftover delicacies as spoon bread. Many interesting people stayed at the hotel, and I had a chance to meet them. One was a millionaire who prided himself on his philanthropy. One woman took off a gorgeous purple orchid and gave it to me when I admired it. "It doesn't mean anything to me," she said. "I have had many." She smiled, "Besides, beautiful flowers are meant for the young."

I learned that boys could be very good friends. One such friend was Eric. He was unassuming, relaxed, witty and fun. I enjoyed being with him. Our conversations ran free and easy. Neither of us tried to impress the other. If we met on the street, we went for a coke. More than once, we pooled our resources, bought one coke, and helped ourselves to two straws.

"Listen," I said one day, feeling rather shy at being so bold. "You know the costume ball where I work is coming in a couple of weeks. If there isn't someone special you want to wait for to ask you, would you go with me? It's not like a date or anything, but I would rather go with you than anyone else."

He grinned, showing his big dimples. He really was cute. "Why, I'd be honored to accept your kind invitation ma'am," he replied in his best Clark Gable manner. "If you're sure you hadn't rather invite somebody more to your liking."

He meant Zack, of course. That is what made our relationship special. He knew my secrets and I knew his. He had a gigantic crush on Peaches. I had decided that unrequited love might make a good story but it was no way to live. "If anything better than you comes along, I won't look," I replied.

Eric was dashing as a pirate. I was less than glamorous in an oldtimey bathing suit, complete with black lisle stockings, my hair tied in a kerchief, and my two front teeth blacked out.

Peaches, a Southern belle, won the contest for best costume, hands down. I won recognition for most original, and my escort won best for male costume. It was an evening to remember, and for more than one reason.

Peaches had been presented with a gardenia corsage by her date. It was a rare and beautiful tribute in our circle of poor friends. After all, Saturday night's movie quite often depended on how many coke bottles or coat hangers you could collect on Friday to sell.

She proudly put the flowers in the window so they would stay fresh. They were lovely.

I awoke in the middle of the night. My entire face itched. My eyes were swollen. I sneezed and my nose ran. I was choking. "Get those things out of here." I tried to scream but my voice was too hoarse to be heard.

I grabbed the blanket from my bed and fled down the hall to the bathroom. I took refuge in the shower stall, but the overhead light glared. Stumbling to the door, I flicked the switch off and groped my way back to the shower, kicking over a can of cleanser that scurried across the floor like one of the roaches that played here in the dark.

"B.J.," she called, shaking my shoulder. "What are you doing in here?"

I blinked at Mindy. "Trying to sleep."

"You can't sleep here."

"Yes, I can." I was getting more and more awake and less and less happy about it.

"Did you and Peaches quarrel?"

"No," I grumped. "It's those dumb flowers."

"You mean you're allergic." She was kneeling close to me. I burst into tears. "I've never been allergic before."

"Well, you can't sleep here."

"Why not?"

"Silverfish and water bugs. Dolly saw a mouse the other night." Anything that creeps, crawls or is small and furry gives me the willies. I had as soon come around a corner and face a lion as a mouse. The lion would kill me but the mouse would frighten me to death.

My blanket and I beat a hasty retreat to the smoking lounge. Nobody was there but Kitty, who was huddled in a big wicker chair in the corner. The light was directly on her book. She was putting in time and a half on the books because she wanted to learn as much as she could before her boyfriend got back from Germany and was released from the Army. They would get married and she would quit school. "Hey, kid," she said. Hers was a deep woman's voice. "Couldn't you sleep?"

"I could but I'm allergic to my roommate's flowers."

"I know about allergies," she said, as she pulled a cigarette from a pack that was open in her lap. "My cousin Pearl is allergic to about everything."

Kitty soon closed her book and went to her room. There was only me and the smell of stale cigarette smoke left.

Thanksgiving holidays were soon there and those who lived close enough were going home. I would spend the holiday on campus while Peaches went home. A dorm is a big and lonely place with most of the kids gone.

67

I sat watching the rain beat on the window pane where it formed teardrops of water before rolling down the glass. "B.J., telephone," the receptionist called. I wasn't expecting a call.

"B.J.," he said. It was Zack. "How about a movie Wednesday night before we take off for the holiday?"

"Why not?" I answered. I wasn't sure whether I had won or lost.

Chapter 14

More Of The Same

Mindy met me in the hall. "Well?"

"We had a good time."

"Did he ask you for another date?"

I started running up the steps. "No." I didn't stop until I got to the first landing, and then I looked over the bannister. "He won't." I felt the tears coming as I ran on up the steps. At the second landing I looked down again. "And he won't."

When Mindy came in, I was laying across the bed crying. I shook with sobs and beat on the pillow.

"Honey, I'm sorry," she said, sitting on the side of the bed.

"Why should you apologize? I was the one who insisted." I sat up and grabbed a Kleenex.

"But, honey, you're one of my best friends, and I can't stand to see you hurt."

Peaches strolled in trailing her coat like Linda Darnell did a mink. "What's with you, B.J."

"Oh!" I moaned.

"There, there, honey," Mindy soothed, with a pat on the shoulder.

"What's wrong with her?" Peaches turned to Mindy.

"Go away," I screeched. I was miserable and maybe dying and my suave, sophisticated roommate was asking stupid questions. She could never understand what agony I was going through.

Mindy suggested, "Why don't you sleep in my room tonight, Peaches?"

Peaches stood in the middle of the floor completely confused. She opened her mouth to speak and then closed it. "OK," she said, slinging her coat on her bed and reaching for her toothbrush and PJ's. "I know when I'm not wanted."

When the door closed behind her, I breathed a sigh.

The door burst open and an outraged Peaches stood there. "Did he try something funny?"

I looked at Mindy and she looked at me. "No," I squeaked.

"Thank God," Peaches said and stepped into the room.

For a few minutes the three of us looked at each other and then it happened. First we smiled and then we grinned. Laughter bounced off the walls. Roars of side-aching sound filled the room, rolled out the door, and went bouncing down the hall. I fell onto the bed doubled over. Mindy dropped to the floor clutching her belly. Peaches hugged the wall.

Neighbors came groggily in rubbing their eyes and reaching for falling curlers. "What's the matter?" they asked. "What's happened?"

"Nothing," one of us managed.

"An inside joke," another got out.

When the lights were out and Mindy was in Peaches' bed and probably half asleep, I said, "Zack's a nice guy. It just didn't work out."

"Maybe it never will," she said and yawned.

I scrunched down in the bed.

"Maybe not," I thought. "But I'm going to keep trying." Then I went to sleep.

The Thanksgiving holiday was quiet. There were no girls singing in the shower or laughing in the halls. I got some studying done.

On Thanksgiving day I got a call from home.

Mamma: How are you?

Me: Fine, and you all?

Mamma: We miss you. (I heard the tremble in her voice.)

Me: I miss you, too.

Mamma: What are you doing?

Me: Eating too much.

70

Mamma: (laugh) Everybody is.

Me: How's the family?

Mamma: (cheerfully) Everybody's fine, but your grandma's had a cold and your daddy's arthritis has been hurting a lot and Lydia nearly had pneumonia, but we're all fine.

Me: I'm sorry.

Mamma: It's just old age, B.J. You don't realize it, but we're getting old.

Me: I don't know what to say to that.

Mamma: That's all right, baby. I'm coming out to see you next weekend.

Me: Say, that's great. Do you have any idea of when you'll get here?

Mamma: No. Does it matter?

Me: Why no, but I wanted to be sure I would be here, that's all.

Mamma: If you aren't there, I'll just wait. I'm not important anyway.

Me: Of course you are.

Mamma: If you don't want me, just say so.

Me: Of course I want you.

Mamma: All right then. I'll see you next weekend. Goodbye, baby. We all love you.

Me: But Mamma — . The line went dead.

I canceled all plans for the next weekend. That should prove that I cared.

"I don't see why she wouldn't tell you when she would get here," Peaches said, as she folded her laundry. "You should have insisted."

Most of my friends were out on Friday evening. I played ping pong for awhile with one of the girls who never went out. "What's the matter, B.J., couldn't you trap some guy to spring the price of a movie?"

"I'd seen the movie," I said, and slammed the paddle in the table and walked away. Why should I tell her?

Back in my room I read the "Readers Digest" from cover to cover and was starting on "Time" by the time Peaches got home. "Has she gotten here yet?"

"No," I said absently.

All the next morning I waited. I read my assignments for Monday's classes. I reviewed my notes. Peaches brought me a hamburger and carton of milk.

I picked out what I would wear to class on Monday and took my shirt to the laundry room and ironed it.

It began to rain outside. Kentucky winters are less than ideal and Corinthe College is in the middle of the nasty weather zone. By four-thirty, it was already getting dark. "Let's go eat and beat the supper line," Peaches suggested.

"Surely she'll be here soon," I said. I was beginning to worry.

"You can always eat twice," she suggested, handing me my raincoat.

When we got back from supper, the girl at the check-out desk said, "B.J., your mother is waiting for you in the parlor."

I rushed in. "Mamma, I'm so glad to see you."

The smile on my face froze. I could tell by the sour expression that something was wrong. I looked around. The only other people in the room were Lois and Timmy woven together like pretzels on the couch. Nobody paid any attention to them.

"Let's go up to the room," I suggested. I would explain that they were engaged.

She rose, tight-lipped. Her glare held twinkles of ice. She followed me without a word. I glanced at Peaches. 'Don't laugh. I know you're getting ready to but don't.' I frowned.

"Well," was Mamma's first word, as she removed her driving gloves. "It seems that you couldn't wait a few minutes for me."

I opened my mouth to speak, but she didn't give me a chance.

"And to have to sit and watch those two," she spluttered. "There were two of them, weren't there?"

I could feel the blood rushing to my face.

"You don't," Peaches said from the closet where she was hanging her raincoat.

"Don't what, young lady," Mamma asked.

"You don't pay any attention to them."

"When all that vulgarity is flaunted right there in front of you, you can't help but see it."

"You don't, if you don't want to," Peaches insisted.

"When I was a girl," Mamma began.

72

I interrupted, "Things have changed."

"Not much," Peaches muttered, picking up her glass with her toothbrush.

"I'll thank you not to interfere when I'm talking to my daughter, young lady," Mamma snapped. She was standing in the middle of the floor. She had not removed her hat or coat.

"Well," Peaches said on her way to the door. "Pardon me." I saw the fire in her eyes.

I touched her arm. "Aren't you going to dinner with us?"

"No thank you," she said and kept going. She slammed the door.

"The handle must have slipped," I said.

"No, it didn't," Mamma said clutching her purse. "That is the most rude young woman it has been my misfortune to meet."

"I like her," I defended.

Mamma sniffed. "You never did have any taste in friends."

"Or anything else," I flared. "Isn't that what you meant?"

"I am your mother and I will not allow you to speak to me like that."

Dinner was grim and almost silent. I did say, "I canceled all of my weekend plans to be with you."

"Why? What are you doing that you don't want me to know about?"

"Nothing," I wailed. "I thought you would be pleased."

"Oh, I am, but I just want you to realize what a sacrifice we are making so you can be here." I knew that my father had spent long periods of time in the VA hospital with arthritis of the spine. He used to say, "I hate to go in there. They take your pants and you can't leave."

Mamma said, "If I had a chance like this, I would really have made something of myself. You're spoiled. Everything's been handed to you."

"I'm working," I defended weakly.

"I don't see waiting on tables as a noble occupation, but then, you don't know how to do anything."

"It's honest work," I said. I was getting a headache. It would be a long weekend.

73

The movie and ball game were both over by the time we got back to the dorm. I was used to the sight of all of the dating couples saying goodnight around the door. They weren't really saying much, but there was a lot going on. I didn't look left or right. It wasn't any of my business what other people did.

"Well, I never!" Mamma said.

"I have," I said and went into the dorm. As I climbed the stairs, I ached in every joint from tension.

Even before I got to the room, I knew Peaches was having one of her temper tantrums. This one was a dilly from the sounds coming from the room.

"You'd better stay with me until she cools off," Mindy suggested.

I shook my head and opened the door. A book barely missed my head and bounced off the opposite hall wall.

Peaches stood with her feet planted apart. She was dressed only in her underwear. She slung her head like a spirited horse with her loose blonde hair cascading over her shoulders. She had her hands on her hips. "The witch," she spat.

I grinned at her. The room was a shambles. I crossed the hall and picked up the book she had thrown. "That's my dictionary," I wailed.

"She had me fooled for awhile, but she really showed her true colors tonight."

"Who?" I asked, knowing perfectly well that she meant Mamma.

She frowned. "You know damned good and well who I mean. The very idea of coming in my room and telling me to shut up."

I closed the door. This might well be a long and hard-fought battle. I handed her the tin cookie box off the shelf. "Here. You seem to be fresh out of things to throw."

I ducked as she bounced the box off the wall. "How do you stand it?" she asked. "She treats you like dirt."

I sank on the side of the bed. "To her, I am forever two years old."

"And she's going to keep treating you that way until you make her stop."

"What do you suggest I do?"

74

"Tell her off," Peaches said, tying her terry robe around her.

"You wouldn't do that."

"If my mamma was like yours, I would."

"No, you wouldn't. You don't say things like that to your mother."

"You're going to have to," she said, shaking her finger at me. "And the sooner, the better."

Later we each lay in our beds in the dark. Neither of us was asleep. "Peaches," I said.

"What?"

"You have an awful mess to clean up tomorrow."

I heard the rustle of her sheets as she turned over. "I got all day."

Mamma left on Sunday evening with the admonition to "Go to church like you were brought up to."

I settled back into my routine of study, dates, visiting with friends and complaining about the food. I also haunted the post office checking my mailbox several times a day.

The first hint of trouble came in a letter from Aunt Lydia:

"Your mother seems to feel that it was a mistake to let you go to college. We will hope the Good Lord has given her enough common sense not to make a mountain out of a mole hill, but I thought it best to warn you, just in case. We love and trust you. You have a great deal of good sense."

This prelude to disaster disturbed me but I could not imagine what terrible thing I had done.

I did not know that the letter that came was to be one of many.

"My Dear Baby,

The trip home was uneventful except for a flat tire halfway home. A very nice young man changed it for me. When your heart is pure, God watches over you.

I was greatly disappointed with the reception I received. You certainly did not seem glad to see me.

(How did I fail? What more could I have done?)

You must have been talking about me to your roommate. She seems to be a nice enough young woman, and the only way I can account for her rudeness is that you have been saying untrue things about me. My mother's heart bleeds when I realize how

75

ungrateful you are. Do what you will, I still love you.

(My God! My God! Tears came to my eyes. Am I like that?)

You may think you have me fooled, but you don't. I know why you didn't want me to meet your friends. You are a brazen hussy, just like the worst of them.

(What is she talking about? I was beginning to feel sick at my stomach.)

If I hadn't been there, you would have been out there in the dark being squeezed like a ripe tomato. Boys don't respect a girl who acts like that. Ask your daddy what men are like. He can tell you. They may play around but when they marry, they look for a good girl.

(I haven't done anything. I am a nice girl.)

We are looking forward to your coming home for Christmas, baby. Remember, we are the only ones you can ever depend on to love you — no matter what.''

I wanted to crawl under a rock and die. How could she say those things? My own mother thought the very worst of me. How could she? What about all the training she had supervised? I felt dirty. Everything was upside down. Your mother is supposed to believe in you when no one else does.

Very slowly, I crawled between the sheets and cried.

Chapter 15

A Sad Sophomore, & After

My second year at Corinth College was not a happy one. I will spare you the details except to say Mamma's letters kept coming and each new one was more scathingly abusive than the one before. It was that year, too that I developed a chronic sinus infection that continues to plague me until today. My self-esteem hit an all time low, and my grades began to plummet. At the end of that year, I packed my bags, shook the Kentucky red clay from my heels and went back to Virginia. What else do you do when you have no money, no job and little education? The one thing I knew for sure was that someday I would get a college degree. I did not know when or how, but someday and somehow I would get a degree.

"I told your Mamma it was a mistake to educate a girl," Daddy said. "They just get married and waste it."

These comforting words from my father led me to raise an eyebrow. "Get married?" Most of the people I knew who were married weren't all that thrilled about it. In fact, I felt sorry for the girls I had known who had either quit school or gotten married as soon as they had graduated. They had small children, tired expressions on their faces and their idea of a big evening was to spend Saturday evening at their parents homes watching wrestling on TV.

The first order of business was to get a job. That might not be so easy to do, since my only office skill was one semester of typing at Corinth College. That did not make me highly qualified to do anything.

My first full-time job was in the district office of a large grocery company. I did not use the typing skill. The job entailed keeping track of merchandise and, in order to do this, we were sent in groups of two or three to Richmond for six weeks of training in the use of the comptometer, an earlier version of a calculator.

The three of us, B.B. Cronan, Millicent Brown, and I met at the Greyhound Bus station at nine o'clock on a hot July morning. There could not have been three young women more different.

B.B. was tall with sandy hair and blue eyes. She was the daughter of a contractor who had settled in our valley after marrying one of our local beauties. B.B. had attended our local hoi-polloi college and then worked as a research assistant for a year afterwards. She said, "I turned in greed and desperation to this job." I soon learned that although she had a Yankee economy of speech, she possessed a beautiful dry sense of humor.

Millicent, on the other hand, was short, and immaculately neat in a well-scrubbed country-girl way. She was engaged to a soldier that she was doggedly faithful to and to whom she wrote every day. She was very religious, reading her well-worn Bible every day and quoting verses from it. As far as I could discern, she had no sense of humor at all. Life was a serious business and not to be frittered away.

There were the three of us eyeing one another and wondering what we were in for in the next six weeks.

"I consider cigarettes a tool of the devil," Millicent declared. "And smoking is a sin."

"I suggest you sit someplace else," I said.

B.B. and I sat together. We discovered that we shared a lot of interests. We both liked boys, reading, music, boys, clothes, money, movies, and, oh yes, boys. We talked the miles away. We shared a love of good food that we did not get at the bus station where we stopped.

78

We saved a visit to the restroom until the last. When I was ready to leave I called, "Come on, B.B."

"Just a minute," she said.

I waited. The voice over the loud speaker announced our bus. "Come on, B.B.," I called more desperately.

"I'll swear," she said.

"What's the matter?"

There was a thrashing noise of elbows hitting the sides of the stall.

"B.B., what's wrong?"

"It's this damn girdle," she said, making more noises. "It's new, and I've sweated so it doesn't want to go up."

"Can I help you?" Our bus was announced again.

"It just isn't going to work," she said.

"Take it off," I suggested. "We're going to miss the bus."

We had to bang on the bus door to get on. B.B. was still muttering about new girdles.

One of our luxuries was a taxi from the bus station to the rooming house where the three of us were to share a top-floor room. It was a colonial brick house on a corner lot beside one of those confederate statues that are dotted throughout the city. "Breakfast is from 6:30 to 8 and dinner is from 5 to 7. If you miss it, you're on your own," the landlady told us. "There's lunch on Saturday, but I do not serve on the Lord's Day."

"Bless you," Millicent said with a smile. "I'm glad to know there are some truly good people in this wicked old world."

I looked at B.B. and she at me. We chose up sides right then. B.B. and I had no intention of letting Millicent's prudery interfere with any good time we might have. We would not be rude, but neither would we be stifled.

The room was large and airy. One advantage was a small balcony. We would spend many steamy evenings out there sitting on that balcony watching the traffic of Richmond go by. I could even go out there and smoke without enduring the glares of the fair Millicent.

We soon settled into a routine. Breakfast at seven, then a bus ride to the building where our school was. After school let out at about 4:30 we quite often walked back to the house. We would window shop on the way. My problem was that I had a pen-

79

chant for spike-heeled shoes and, more often than not, I limped the last few blocks while I emitted groans and complaints.

Some of the other people in the boarding house we seldom saw and did not get to know. There must have been 15 of us in all. We did get to know one young man from Pennsylvania. His company had transfered him to Richmond. He sometimes ate dinner at our table, and one evening he asked, "Would you girls like to go for a ride?"

B.B. and I did not have to be coaxed. We knew he had a convertible.

"I don't know if it would be proper," Millicent protested.

"He isn't asking for a date," B.B. said.

"We'll be there to protect your virtue," I added.

"Well, I guess it will be all right."

"Suit yourself," I said, as I got up from the table. She had been invited, just like we had.

It soon became apparent that Bill, that was his name, was showing off his harem to his friends. We co-operated by talking about good old Bill as though we had known him forever.

When we got back to our room, Millicent enthused, "I had such a good time. William is such a nice man."

"Just stick with us," B.B. said. "You ain't seen nothing yet."

B.B. and I talked about the evening conversation with Bill.

"That's not his name," Millicent interrupted.

"OH?" B.B. and I intoned together.

"I distinctly remember him saying his name was William."

I looked at B.B. She was rolling her eyes back in her head.

"Oh for goodness sake, Millicent; just read your Bible."

"Why? What did I say wrong?"

B.B. couldn't stand it any longer. She rolled over on the bed and convulsed with laughter.

I fought for control. "You see," I said. "The nickname for William is Bill."

"Oh." She smiled wanly.

"Now do you understand?"

"I guess so."

Our lives began to brighten when we asked our teacher what there was to do outside of school. "A lot of my girls enjoy going out to the Army camp and to the Y-sponsored dances." We looked askance. "Now listen, there isn't any funny stuff. The dances are chaperoned, and the rules are very strict. Any girl caught breaking any of the rules is not allowed to go back. You ride out and back on a bus and stay with the group.

Even Millicent decided to go to at least one dance. We had nothing to lose but an evening. We met the other girls at the bus. They were a mixture of store clerks, secretaries and students. Spirits were high.

"Heh, Maxine," one girl called to another. "Do you reckon that clown who walked all over your feet last week will be back for round two this week?"

"Jesus, I hope not," came the reply.

"He can walk on my feet anytime," someone else said.

"Tilley, you never did have any taste,"

Maxine laughed. "He dances like he's still following that plow out in Iowa."

"Say, you're new, aren't you?" the girl next to me asked.

"Yes," I said. "Does it show?"

"No," she said pertly. "I just don't remember seeing you before." She lit a cigarette.

"Watch out for the pinchers. The patters aren't so bad but the pinchers are something else," she warned.

It is a sure bet that no girl sat out a dance at one of those dances unless she wanted to. Each dance was with a different partner. Some were tall and some were short. Accents came from all over. Then I danced with Ted and no one else. He was an excellent dancer and extremely good looking, with olive complexion, big brown eyes, and black hair. We liked each other. "You'll be back next week?" he asked, as he helped me on the bus.

"Maybe," I answered, knowing that only illness could keep me away.

He pulled me into his arms and kissed me. "I'll be back," I said.

"I'll be waiting for you," he said.

B.B. asked, "Who was the cute guy?"

"His name is Ted and he's from New York. Why?"

"Nothing but he's cute — and the way he looked at you!"

81

I grinned in the dark. "There is nothing like being appreciated." Ted and I both knew that the fact that we met at all was a minor miracle. We also knew that he was subject to transfer and that with each passing week my time in Richmond was running out. This added pleasure to each date because we were amassing memories. If we never saw each other again, and we did not, we had those memories and those good times to remember.

"I felt like a loose woman," Millicent declared.

"For someone so religious, you have quite a vocabulary," I observed.

"Yeah," B.B. said. "How did you know so much?"

"Why, they have them in the Bible."

It was our last week of school when our teacher called us into her office. "You girls are the best I have in this class. I have an employer here in Richmond who is anxious to give you jobs."

"We couldn't do that," Millicent said. For once I agreed with her.

"It would be unethical for us to quit after our company gave us this training," I said. I sometimes wonder how different all of our lives would have been if we had taken her up on this offer.

"But don't you see," our teacher said. "Your company has lied to you. The comptometer company has trained you because your company buys their machines from us. Your schooling hasn't cost them a red cent."

"They paid our room and board," B.B. said.

"Girls," the teacher said. "I am willing to help you better your lot, if you will let me. Your company is not a good one and you will learn that. I am trying to help you avoid that pain."

We shook our heads. What was right and honest was all we could think of.

"They told you that there was room for advancement in their company, didn't they?"

"Yes, they did," Millicent said. "How did you know?"

"I have worked with them for years. What they mean is that there is room for advancement, if you are a man."

"The manager of our office started out as a truck driver."

The teacher smiled. "What about that woman who has been sitting at the same desk for the past 25 years?"

There was one we knew, but she seemed to be so happy.

We finished out our week, packed our bags, and, wrapped in our integrity, headed for home and our grubby little jobs.

Ted wrote to me and I wrote to him until Mamma ran across my letters from him. "Hussy," she called me. "You're just a common pick-up."

"Stay out of my mail. If I could, I'd prosecute you. Reading somebody else's mail is the most low down, mean thing you could do," I screamed.

"I am your mother, and you are not to talk to me that way."

"I'm warning you. Stay out of my mail."

"You will not speak to me like that and you will have no more discourse with that man."

The one good thing about the whole episode was B.B. We were friends and companions for a long time. We took classes together. We saw "The Red Shoes" and "The Tales of Hoffman" together. We painted pictures. We tramped through the woods on Sunday afternoons.

Mamma said, "I don't see why you like B.B. so much. She doesn't talk much, and she puts ketchup on her eggs."

"She's my friend, Mamma. Leave her alone." I meant it and that was one time Mamma shut up.

Chapter 16

Old Friends & New

Love, Mindy style, was not something she told me about. She showed me. Her husband, Cal, was a professional forester and her son, Mack, was a baby acrobat.

There was one bus a week into the town where she lived and one bus out. They met me at the service station where the bus stopped just long enough for me and my suitcase to get off.

From where I sat in the kitchen watching Mindy put the finishing touches on our evening meal. I could see into the living room where Mack was asleep in his playpen with his diapered rump stuck up in the air. He had his thumb stuck in his mouth and would occasionally wake just enough to suck in contentment.

This was the closest I had ever been to a baby, and I was fascinated. I had thought of babies in terms of burdens. They had to be clothed and fed, and kept you from doing what you wanted to. But this baby was real. He was cuddly and sweet and had all those moving parts, like arms and legs, and an excellent sprinkler system.

"Here," Mindy said earlier, holding him toward me. "Hold him while I get a fresh diaper."

My expression must have been less than enthusiastic because she laughed. "For goodness sake, B.J., he won't break. He is very bendable. He is washable and also drip dry. What better qualifications does he need?"

There was something magic about sitting there holding Mack in my arms. He was a little trusting person and, despite what Mindy said, I held him very carefully. What does one say to a baby anyway? I settled for, "Hi, guy." Maybe I was wrong. There might be a lot to be said for having a home of your own and a husband who loved you and a sweet child.

Daddy wouldn't even let me get an apartment of my own. "You have a perfectly good home," he said.

"But, Daddy, it would be so nice to have a place of my very own."

"What do you want to do in an apartment that you can't do here?" he asked.

All that I could think of to say was, "Sleep late on Saturdays."

When I announced that I was going to teach dancing to earn a living, both my parents showed their displeasure in no uncertain terms. "That's the craziest idea I've ever heard."

I did teach that winter, but had to go back to office work when my boss insisted all instructors go to New York to study that summer. I had already developed my life-long love of clothes, books, and records. As my collections grew, my finances shrank. For most of us, it is true that you can have money or other things, but not both.

So I sat at Mindy's kitchen table contentedly sipping black coffee and smoking while her baby slept and she was busy making thousand island dressing.

The process was fascinating. It had never occurred to me that you could make salad dressing or to wonder at what was in it. I thought you went to the store and picked up a bottle of your choice, went home, emptied it, and then threw the bottle away.

"Zack is in the Army in Japan," she said, as she chopped boiled eggs. "Right after he graduated from Corinth, he enlisted."

I should have been warned of what was coming next from the expression on her face. It was her matchmaker look. "Say," she said, brushing a wisp of hair with the back of her hand. "Maybe you ought to write to him."

I smiled, "I thought you were the one who said Zack and I could never got along."

"Well," she said, tilting her head to one side. "Maybe both of you have changed."

Whatever that statement was supposed to mean, I do not know. However, when I got home and unpacked my bag, I found Zack's address neatly tucked inside. The happy little matchmaker also sent my address to Zack so that our letter to each other crossed somewhere in the Pacific. We began our new relationship with a great deal of caution. Neither of us was in any hurry for anything but the most casual friendship. He told me things about Japan that you do not read in "National Geographic," and I wrote him about the latest additions to my various collections and about the book I was reading at the time

Our letters became more heated and more frequent when we got in a long distance argument over whether George Washington or Thomas Jefferson was the greater man. I wrote, "After all, Washington was the father of our country."

He wrote back, "He sure was."

By the time Zack was getting ready to return to the states, we were writing and receiving letters every day. A day without a letter was a day lost.

In one letter he wrote: "All I have ever wanted to do is teach in college. I will go to the University this fall if Big Uncle will let me out of the Army early. I have been accepted in graduate school."

Big Uncle did not cooperate, and Zack missed the fall semester. What he did was go visit his family and what he did then was to come by my house for a brief visit befor going on to Baltimore to stay with his brother in a trailer and work at the aircraft factory.

What he also did was kiss me goodbye before he left. The bells went off and the rockets did flare. I was not sure how things were different between us or even why, but they were.

What I didn't know until much later was that I was not the only girl he stopped to see on that trip. By the time I did find out, it didn't matter.

Every weekend he drove down from Baltimore. Every day we wrote to each other. If, for one reason or another, he could not make the weekly pilgrimage, we had long, and expensive, telephone calls.

We found each other's actions and ideas of great interest. Life took on new meaning with someone to share it.

Zack was saving as much as possible of what her earned for graduate school. I found myself more and more frequently in linen and china departments on my lunch hour.

Because we had other places for our money to go, we did not eat at fancy restaurants or go anyplace else that required much money. We did spend so much time in one coffee shop that it felt like home. We also spent a lot of time at the airport watching planes land and take off.

It was a cold, rainy winter evening and we were sitting in the car smoking and listening to the music on the car radio. I could still hear the words ringing in my ears the waitress back at the coffee shop had whispered to me as we were leaving, "Why don't you two get married and cut out all this nonsense?"

Get married? How could we get married? Each of us was doing well to take care of himself. Zack would go to the University in January, and I had the highest paying and least work job I had ever had. The whole idea was unthinkable.

"You sure are quiet this evening," he said. He still worries about me if I don't talk much.

"Have you seen Mindy lately?" I asked.

"No." Zack put his arms around me. "As far as I know, she doesn't know about us."

"I sure haven't told her," I said.

We stopped talking to listen to a song we liked. When the song was over, Zack said, "When are you coming down to meet my family?"

It was a question that had to be answered. I knew such a little about them except what Zack had told me. His father was a farmer and his mother was a good farm wife. Zack was the youngest of five children. "Whenever it will suit them for me to come," I replied.

Zack and I cooked up a surprise for Mindy. I wrote her:

"I had such a good time the last time I was there, that I am coming for another visit."

Again I rode the once-a-week bus. Zack drove to his home some 30 miles away. I was so nervous I could not sit still. Every time a car went past her house, I jumped. At last, I heard a car pull in her drive and stop. "I think I'll go out for a little fresh air."

"You'd better put on a sweater," she warned. "That mountain air is cold."

I didn't have time to follow her advice.

"I thought something funny was going on," Mindy greeted us when we walked in her kitchen. That sparkle was in her eyes again. "Tell me all about it," she said. We told her as much as we wanted her to know.

"You'll get along all right with all of them but maybe Rachel. She's Zack's oldest sister, and she tends to be a little snippy sometimes. Just don't let her hurt your feelings and you'll be all right."

The closer we got to Zack's house, the more jittery I got. "What if they don't like me?"

"What's there not to like?" he said, and then he added. "They did want to know why I hadn't settled for one of the local girls."

"Oh," I moaned.

"Quit worrying," he said.

"What about Rachel? Mindy said there might be a problem there."

"There won't be. Just be yourself."

"Right now, I wish I could be somebody else," I wailed.

When he opened the car door for me, I said. "My knees are shaking so bad I don't know if I can stand up or not. Do I look all right? Is my hair OK? Let's go back."

"Don't be silly," he said, pulling me to my feet. "They're nice people. I'm their son, and you're rather fond of me, aren't you?"

He pulled me to him and kissed me. The rockets went off and the bells went clang. One of us sure had learned a lot since college.

Mindy was dead wrong. Rachel and I liked each other at once. She put forth every effort to put me at ease. Through the years she has remained a trusted and true friend. I have never had a problem too petty for her to help. When Zack was in graduate school, she sent me an occasional gift of clothing with a note saying something like, "Thought this would look good on you." For at least a few days, I walked taller. She has been the sister I never had, and she is one of my favorite people. She can be a "no nonsense" person with a caustic tongue but I've got her number called. She's really a marshmallow, a pussycat, and not a tiger.

My future in-laws were beautiful people. My father-in-law was over six feet tall with a shock of white hair and broad shoulders. He had a sense of humor and an insistance on justice. He was a God-fearing, good man. We were friends from the very beginning. "I see why Zack chose you," he greeted me. "My son has very good taste." You have to love a man like that.

My future mother-in-law was as short as I am. She was not a little woman in spirit and love. She had more compassion than anyone I had ever met. There was room on her lap for any child and space in her heart to share love with all humans. She also was a worry wart. When Zack was sent into the Army, she cried but not because she would miss him, but because she was afraid, "He won't like it."

"She was right," Zack said. "I didn't."

That weekend we also visited Zack's brother, Jay, and his wife, Virginia, in their new home. It was so new, there were no walks in yet. Although the part of the country I came from was thinking spring, this part of the mountains still had snow and bitter winds. After the sun went down, the snow that melted in the daytime froze.

We were invited for dinner. "Don't forget which of us you're engaged to," Zack said. "He is good looking."

Jay was good looking, but no more so than Zack. His wife was a very nice person and a terrific cook. We got along well. I even managed to behave with some dignity until we left.

We had put our coats on and were headed for the car. My feet hit the ice on the boards that bridged the mud where the walk would be. My feet were going and I splattered mud in all directions

Zack turned and did not hesitate. He laughed.

89

I struggled to get up, but only managed to slide even deeper in the mud.

"Are you hurt?" Virginia asked. She and Jay had come out of the house. Jay was laughing too.

"I'm fine," I said. "This is just a beauty bath."

"You look so funny." Zack said.

"And you're acting like a husband already."

"I'm sorry," he said, wiping the tears. "But you ought to see yourself."

"I guess I do look pretty silly."

"That's what you get for trying to be so pretentious."

I was tempted to pull him down in the mud, too, when he reached out to help me, but I was afraid they might not let me in the family if I mistreated baby brother.

When we got in the car, Zack said, "I'm sorry, honey, but you looked so," he started to laugh again.

"Well, nothing got wounded by my pride."

"I'll never forget the expression on your face."

"I hope you have a long memory, because I don't plan on entertaining you by rolling around in the mud very often.

And that was my introduction to the family I was marrying into. They were religious and sometimes irreverent. Their lives were spent in hard work and that is what they expected. They saw humor in the every day. They were what would be called 'good people'. I loved them all and we share respect. What more could you ask for?

Chapter 17

The Degree

Our apartment was half of an old house. Our landlady was a retired registrar of the school I was attending. She lived in one half of the house and we lived in the other. She was a thin-lipped old lady who relied more and more on Zack to perform any duty she felt that you kept a man around the house for. He was too much of a gentleman to refuse, although sometimes things became a bit tedious. She was a very religious person who did not allow alcohol on the property, and so it was with surprise that Zack asked, "Do you smell beer?"

I sniffed the air, not believing what I smelled. "Do you guess she bought some new perfume and doesn't know what it is?"

Our question was answered when Miss Ida called us into her apartment. She looked very sheepish. The smell was definitely beer.

"My beautician said that she thought if she rinsed my hair in beer it might give more body." She smiled. "Of course, I could not buy it for myself, so I asked the man who works on my car to get it for me." She blushed. "He couldn't help but tease me by waiting until I was talking to the dean and then calling as loud as he could, 'I have your beer for you, Miss Ida.' I was so embarrassed."

"That explains how it got here," Zack said. "But what happened to it?"

"I'm getting to that," she said. "I brought it home and put it in the refrigerator but when I took it out it seemed so cold, I decided to warm it just a little bit."

"How did you do that?" I asked.

"I put it in a pan of water and slipped it into the oven. The oven wasn't very warm, and I never dreamed anything like this would happen."

"Did you take the lid off?" Zack asked.

"Oh dear, was I supposed to take the lid off?"

"Yes, ma'am."

"My word, then that explains why it blew up. I had to wash my curtains and the floor and everything. What I wanted to ask you is how can I get it off the ceiling?"

I couldn't stand it, so I used the old 'I gotta go' routine and went upstairs to the bathroom and laughed until I cried.

On an evening not long afterward, I was in the bedroom when I heard a noise in the closet in the next room. Zack's clothes and our moving boxes were in there, as well as some old cans on the window sill left there by the previous tenants. I went to investigate. How strange. I had never noticed that cable coming out of the eaves before. It came out of the side of the wall and lay across the window and stuck straight out a couple of inches on the other side.

Zack was across the hall in the bathroom. "Zack," I called. "Will you come here a minute."

"What's up?" he asked. He still had the towel in his hand.

"It's strange. All the time we have lived here, I never noticed that cable before."

He said, "Me either."

"You stand right here," Zack said and went to get a flashlight. When he got back, he flashed the beam on the cable. There were two black eyes looking back at us.

"What if we hadn't been upstairs?" I asked.

"Then one fine morning when I went to put on my coat, I would have a surprise. You stand right here with the flashlight. I'll go get a hoe."

I held the light and looked at the snake. He looked at me. Neither of us moved. I don't know about him, but I was too scared to breathe.

Zack came back with the hoe and a box. "That son-of-a-gun must be six feet long. You can't even see his tail." He put the box down. "You hold the light and I'll kill him."

I nodded. My hands were beginning to shake.

When Zack took the first swing, that snake leaped off the wall full length. I dropped the flashlight and turned tail and ran. There are some times in life when you are purely on your own. I could hear Zack chopping and cussing.

Then all was silent. I stood outside the door and wondered who had won. I waited for the winner to emerge. Why, I might be a widow at the very moment.

"It's OK," Zack called, "Come out wherever you are."

"Did you kill him?" I asked.

"At least 40 times," he said holding out the box. "See."

"I don't want to see. Just get rid of him."

Zack rolled his eyes. "It's just a black snake. You are the biggest coward I've ever seen."

"I sure am," I said. "And I plan on being a live coward for a very long time."

Someone asked me not long ago, what I had learned from that experience. I said, "I learned just how fast old B.J. could run. That's what I learned, and I'll give you odds I set a record."

Our lives revolved around our schools. It was Zack's first college teaching job, and he was working harder than his students. He was so sincere!

My college did not demand too much of me. I did. I had just watched Zack put forth his best effort in graduate school, and I intended to do no less. I wanted to learn as much as I could. I devoured what was offered ferociously.

"For goodness sake, my dear," my English professor told me. "Slow down. Nothing is going away. You don't have to learn everything today."

In my Shakespeare class, another professor asked, "B.J., why didn't Hamlet stab the king from behind the curtains?"

It had been a dull class right after lunch and the room was too warm. "Because Shakespeare was writing a five-act play and this is only act three," I said.

93

My life was a patchwork of classes and textbooks. I went after education with a vengeance. It was the first time I studied because I wanted to know. The world opened up for me.

One teacher often said, "When you are in Paris, I want you to look for this. Notice, I do not say 'if' but 'when' because you are living in a world where travel abroad is not reserved for the wealthy. All I ask is that you conduct yourselves as you would at home." I wondered if she had ever seen people at a convention. "Do not be an ugly American." I laughed. There might be some who would travel but I would never get outside the country.

Years later Zack said, "We're going to Ireland."

He went two weeks before the children, then 11, 5 and just turned 3-year-old joined him for six weeks. I laughed all the way there and back. But then, that's another story.

Some of Zack's colleagues became lifetime friends. I will never forget the first time we had Zack's department head and his wife out to dinner. I was very nervous. The silver was polished and the china gleamed. Phil and Cathy noticed I was sitting on the edge of my chair.

"What are you going to do with your degree, B.J.?" Phil asked.

"I'm not really sure," I replied. "Right now, I'm just excited about all of those things I don't know. Maybe I'll be a professional student."

"Do you want to teach?" Cathy asked. That subject always came up. You were a secretary, a nurse or a teacher. Why else would you get an education?

I shook my head. They were trying very hard to put me at ease. "No," I said. "I'll leave the teaching to Zack. Besides, I don't know anything about children."

"They're delightful," Cathy said. They had a young daughter who was very bright.

"Hm," Phil said, sucking on his pipe. "B.J., if you could do anything you wanted to do, what would it be?"

I lit another cigarette. "I'd write," I said. I frowned. "The only problem is that I knew a writer one time, and he said you had to 'live' before you can write. Somehow I can't see me going through husbands like Scarlett O'Hara running a gunboat."

94

They both laughed. Phil said, "Hm, again, and added, "I can't see you doing those things either, but what do you want to write? There are all kinds of writing, you know. I rather like the short story myself."

"Oh, I don't know. I like fiction and I love a good story."

"How about poetry?" he asked.

"Oh, I could never do that."

"It doesn't have to rhyme."

"I know, but it reveals so much about the poet."

"You can't have it both ways, B.J. First you say you aren't sure you have anything to say and then you turn right around and say you don't want to say too much. You have to make up your mind."

"Oh," was all I could think of to say. I had been caught on the horns of my own dilemma.

"Think about it," he said, tapping the tobacco out of his pipe.

We went in to dinner. All went well and I began to relax.

"Anyone for dessert?" Zack said. "B.J. makes a good devil's food cake."

"That sounds daring enough," Phil said.

"That was a very good dinner," Cathy said.

I smiled at the praise and got the dessert plates. They were a wedding gift from Jay and Virginia. Just about everything we had was a wedding gift.

I wished I could drop through the floor when I took the lid off the cake holder. There was my lovely cake with the top layer sliding off the lower one.

Cathy looked from the sloppy cake to my face and then began to laugh. The others joined in. After Zack's praise, I felt like I was smaller than a gnat.

When Zack could stop laughing long enough, he said, "That's OK, B.J. It will taste all right."

"Yes," Phil said. "Don't keep your cockeyed cake all to yourself."

"You are being rather selfish, B.J.," Cathy agreed.

It was only then I could laugh with them.

You may never get rich teaching, but you meet some interesting people, like Padraic Colum. I fell madly in love with the little Irishman when Zack and I picked him up at the airport. He had two questions: "Where is the Catholic Church?" and, "if you have no pubs, where do you drink and where do you get it?" He was a leprechaun of a man with music in his voice.

I had a question for him. "Is it true that the Irish eat as many potatoes as they're reported to?"

He chuckled and patted me on the hand. "Oh, yes, and it's true, and we drink as much as we're reported to, also."

In the spring of our school year, Zack and I had a serious talk. "I love teaching," he said. "But if I stay in college teaching, I need a Ph.D."

"If that is what you want, that's what we will do."

"I'm going to the university Saturday and talk to my advisor."

The day before summer school started was no time to get sick. I had to register for classes no matter how I felt. I only lacked about 12 hours to complete my degree. I blamed my malaise on the heat. I dragged myself home and went to sleep on the couch.

When I awoke I could smell cabbage, carrots and celery cooking in the landlady's apartment. 'Oh' I thought. I rushed up the steps to the bathroom. That is where Zack found me lying on the floor with the cool tile next to my cheek.

"What's wrong?" he said.

"Nothing much," I replied weakly. "I'm just dying, that's all."

"No you're not," he said.

"Fat lot you know about it," I said. "I've turned inside out several times."

He got a wet wash cloth. "Here. This will make you feel better."

"Nothing will make me feel better but dying and getting it over with."

He sat on the side of the tub. "Do you want something to eat?"

I groaned. "I don't ever want to see food again. I think I've been poisoned already."

96

"No, you haven't," he said.

We sat in silence. He just looked at me. I was sick again.

"Say, you are sick," he said.

"That's what I've been trying to tell you," I moaned.

"Come on," he said, pulling me by the arm. "You can't just lie there. Come on, I'll put you in the bed."

"It doesn't matter whether I die here or in bed."

"Oh, for pity's sake," he said, and picked me up and took me into the bedroom.

Once between the cool sheets and in my soft gown, I felt a little better. Zack sat on the side of the bed and held my hand. "Promise me something," I said.

"What?"

"Promise you'll bury me in pink. You always liked me in pink."

He didn't answer; he just laughed.

"I'm serious and when I'm gone you'll be sorry you laughed."

He wiped his eyes with the back of his hand. "You're not dying and I think I know what's wrong with you. If you stop and think, you'd know too."

"I'm too sick to think," I said, but I knew. I wish I could say that was the only miserable day I had. It wasn't so much that I had morning sickness but more like the 24-hour laments. All I could eat and keep down were fresh peaches. Zack brought them to me by the baskets full. I dragged to classes and came home to my couch of pain. I prepared my lessons lying flat on my back and in small doses.

After my first visit to the doctor I called Mamma. "I'm pregnant." How beautiful those words sounded.

"This baby will complicate things," Zack said. "But I guess babies always do."

"I'm sorry," I said.

"What are you apologizing for? I'm not exactly an innocent bystander."

The doctor gave me pills for nausea. We decided to celebrate our new role of parents-to-be by having steak. Nothing ever smelled better than that steak cooking. My mouth watered. It was cooked to perfection. I carefully cut a piece and put it in my

97

mouth and started to chew. It was awful. I put it in a napkin. "That meat is rotten."

"No, it's not," Zack said, putting another piece in his mouth.

"It is too."

"No, it's not," he said.

I sat and watched him eat all of his steak and then reach for mine. "No need to let a perfectly good piece of meat go to waste."

"You're the meanest man in the world," I said and burst into tears.

"No, I'm not," he said. "But we fathers-to-be have to keep up our strength."

I went to the refrigerator and got a peach.

When my summer school was over, Zack backed the U-Haul to the door and we headed back to the university. By that time Zack was calling me "little mother," and I was waddling like a duck when I walked.

Chapter 18

Granny

The house was in an old neighborhood. It had been a mill house far from a solid shield against the outside winds. "If B.J. hadn't been pregnant that winter, she would have frozen to death," Zack said.

However, the rooms were large and there were lots of windows. It came furnished with a refrigerator, stove, and (joy of joys) there was a washing machine.

Mamma came down to help us get settled. "You have no business doing all that bending and lifting, in your condition."

I was allowed to direct traffic and unload dishes from boxes that Zack put on the table.

Mamma cleaned the kitchen cabinets, lined them with shelf paper, and said, "I'll get the lower ones after lunch."

We ate our bologna sandwiches. I put the dishes in the sink and had my back to Mamma. I heard her open the cabinet.

"I've never seen anything so filthy in all my life."

"What is it?" I asked, looking over her shoulder. The shelves were invisible under layers of dead roaches. "Good grief," I said.

Mamma rolled up her sleeves "Just get out of the way. I couldn't sleep a wink in this house, knowing those things were here."

"At least, they're dead."

"I don't care if they are. I want them out of here."

99

I went back to my job and left Mamma to her dust pan, brush and roll of paper towels. She was saying unkind things under her breath about some people's living habits. I was unprepared for her scream.

I jumped. "What in the world — ," I began, but then I saw at her feet what had once been a mouse. "I think I'm going to be sick," I said.

"You'll have to race me." She headed out the door. I touched it.

The bathroom was a closed-in corner of the back porch. There was no insulation. We had to keep the shower curtain pulled all winter to keep from freezing, even with an electric heater. One spark in the old house and we would be lucky to escape with out lives.

After Mamma went to all that trouble to clean that cabinet, I could never bring myself to use it.

It did not take us long to get settled into our new home. This time we were even poorer since I did not work. That left the G.I. bill and Zack's salary as assistant teacher at the university. Money was so tight we couldn't afford an occasional movie. "I'll have room for a garden next spring," Zack said. The trick was to survive until then.

On the evening after Mamma left, we had our first visitor. She was a tiny woman, coming barely to my shoulder, with bright blue eyes and salt and pepper hair in a neat permanent. She wore an immaculate house dress and she wore an apron. She was Granny from next door. She stayed no longer than thirty minutes, but we learned that she was 64 years old, had been married twice ("If you ask me, an old woman that marries an old man is a fool. Take me, for instance, I can come and go as I please and stay as long as I want to and don't have nobody to take care of when I get home. Now, if I had some old man that some other woman's already got all the good out of, things sure would be different."), that she had three children, two of whom lived in town, and that, "I'm an old snuff dipper. You'll get used to it." She carried a clean tomato can with a Kleenex in it, "I'll see you tomorrow. You won't have a thing to worry about," she said, patting my hand. "I know all about babies,

100

Lord love them. They're the biggest blessing God will ever give you."

"What happened?" Zack asked, after she left.

"You have just met a connoisseur of conversation," I said. "And if you don't mind, I'm going take my little blessing," I patted my tummy, "and go to bed."

"I have to stay up and study." That phrase was as familiar at our house as "Good morning."

What we didn't know was that we had been adopted. She brought us goodies, like a jar of her very own blackberry jelly or a dried-apple pie, or a package of frozen strawberries. "They're too much for one old woman like me," she said, but I knew she had heard me talk about how much I would like to have a strawberry shortcake.

She checked on me everyday. "My but you look fine today," she said, and then she laughed. "If you make it 'til January, like that doctor says, it'll be a miracle."

Mamma and Aunt Lydia gave me a gift. It was a sewing machine. On it, I made all of my maternity clothes. As the fall ran out and the cold weather descended with a vengeance, I kept sewing. I haunted fabric shop sales, usually buying seconds or remnants. I made bibs for the baby and Christmas gifts, since there would be no money for gifts.

One bitter cold day, Granny pecked on the back door about 11:30. "Why don't you come over and have lunch with me! It won't be much; just some macaroni and cheese, and a few beans." She forgot to mention the slaw and the biscuits that melted in your mouth.

In addition to our sharing food and conversation, I got warm. It was a delicious treat to be gloriously warm.

"That old house over there," Granny said, pointing to where I lived. "It gets cold, doesn't it?"

"Sometimes," I admitted. "But I try to stay busy."

"Don't you stay over there and get cold, honey. My door is always open and you are welcome any time."

"You are very kind," I said.

"Kind nothing. I wouldn't want one of my girls to be over there, and you're just like one of mine. I mean it. You come over here or I'm going to get mad."

After that, on cold afternoons, I would take my handwork over to Granny's. We talked and worked. She pieced quilts while I sewed on buttons or put in hems in baby clothes.

"This little town hasn't always been dead like it is now. Back during the war, there was a nitro plant here, and both my girls worked there. I kept some roomers, too. The mister didn't like it much, but I says to him, I says, 'You don't complain when it comes to spending the money,' and he shut up. You've got to tell 'em once in awhile." She paused to spit in her cup. "There was several different ones stayed here at one time or another. Some of them comes to see me once in awhile. Lou comes by every chance she gets. I expect you'll meet her sometime. She never married but she's got a good job now. She stayed home and took care of her mamma until she died. Funny how there's always one willing to do that, to stay on and let the others lead their own lives."

I moved around in the chair getting more comfortable.

"Others, you never see again. Misty was like that, but I'm glad I helped her what I could. I've never seen a body needed somebody to care as much as she did. She was little and skinny, with long stringy blonde hair. Poor little thing looked like she hadn't had a good meal in a month. She worked real hard but you could tell it was awful. I made up my mind right there and then that I was going to bring her home for supper. 'I got a baby at the sitter's,' she said. 'Bring him along' I says. 'It's a her,' she says. 'That's fine with me,' I says."

She spat again and wiped her mouth with a neatly folded tissue. "Well," she said. "It turned out the poor girl was an orphan and didn't have a decent place to live. She stayed here about six months with that baby. You should have seen that baby grow. She was a darling child and I loved her, too. Misty met one of those young soldiers over at the University and they hit it off from the start. Well, the first thing you know, she has stars in her eyes and he's over here every minute he can find."

She paused for a minute and cocked her head to one side. "She and this young man got married. I kept the baby so they could go to the beach for a honeymoon. When they get back, he had orders that he's being transferred to Texas, and they take the baby and they go. She said she'd write but she never did."

The room was so quiet you could hear the clock tick. "That's the way it is sometimes. You give of yourself for a time and then you're parted. It's the quality of the giving that counts, though. Don't you think so, honey?"

I blinked back tears. How beautiful she was. That's what being a Christian is, seeing a need and not waiting to be asked to help. "Yes, Granny," I said. "That's what counts."

That year, Christmas sneaked up on us in cold-wet dampness. We packed our bags for our usual visit home.

"B.J.," Mamma said. "You shouldn't be traveling in your condition."

"We thought we ought to make the trip. After the baby comes, we want to spend Christmas at home with him or her."

"Well, B.J., we always stayed home with you for Santa," Daddy said.

"Of course," Zack said, "This baby will not make any difference in our lifestyle. B.J. and I both are career people."

My father laughed. "Of course not," he said, but there was something unbelieving in his tone.

We delivered the same message in the mountains at New Year's, which didn't seem to shake them up too much. "We'll miss you," they said.

There was a lot of rain in January. I had plenty of time to watch it. The first nine months of carrying a baby is not so bad, but every day thereafter seems like an added month. "You look like one of those plastic dolls that is weighted so that, when you knock it over, it rolls upright," Mamma said, and that was when I was about seven months pregnant.

"The only problem is that, if I fell over, I'd stay for a week.

"You can go to the hospital now, B.J.; grandma Rachel is here."

We played honeymoon bridge and double solitaire. The days melted by, and it was all I could do to get up out of a chair. I looked awful and was beginning to feel guilty for not co-operating when everyone was being so nice.

"You still here?" Granny would say each morning.

Mamma called every night. "Are you sure everything's ok and the doctor just isn't telling you?"

"I thought of that," I said. Mamma was such a comfort.

Rachel went home and my in-laws came. Mom took charge immediately. She did the cooking and the washing. She scrubbed floors and ironed. "Your only job right now is to have that baby," she said.

"You just make sure you bring home a granddaughter. I have two grandsons and I want another granddaughter," my father-in-law said.

"I'll bring home anything I can," I said. "Just so I can go someplace to get him."

"Her," he corrected.

February 7th dawned cold and clear. In the afternoon Mom and I went to visit Granny. She walked and I waddled. "You're going to have that baby tomorrow," Granny said. "That's your present to me on my sixty-fifth birthday."

"I'm going to be pregnant forever," I wailed. It took Mom on one side of the chair and Granny on the other to pry me up.

When Mamma called that night, she said, "I wish you would hurry up and have that baby." She added, "I've had my bag packed for three weeks, and I'm running out of clean underwear." Clean underwear has always been a big item in our family. "What would happen if you had a wreck and had to go to the hospital in dirty underwear?" Heaven forbid! Such a possibility brought to mind unheard-of shame. There are some things nice people just don't do.

When Zack left with me for the hospital, my father-in-law woke up long enough to say. "Remember now, B.J., a granddaughter."

The three days in the hospital seemed an age. I could hardly wait to get home with my baby. Just like all other mothers with their first born, I sometimes felt like I was a little girl again playing with my doll, but this doll cooed and smiled and did baby things.

My father-in-law greeted me with, "She's just what I ordered." He would sit by her crib with a smile on his face and watch her sleep.

Granny came down to see the new arrival and declared she had the makings of a real beauty. She brought Linda a quilt that she had made especially for her. "She is something special to me, being born on my birthday."

When Linda was a little over two months old, I had to go back to work. Granny would take care of Linda. Zack would take her to Granny's house while I finished getting ready for work. If the weather was bad, he left me crying because I had to leave her. I vowed that if I had another child, I would not leave my baby with someone else to keep.

The months did pass, and at last school was out and we prepared for another move. "How would you like to buy a house, B.J.?" Zack said one evening.

"I would love to," I said. "It will give us the feeling of having roots."

The house we bought was small, but we thought it was the most beautiful house anyone had ever had. It was new and it was ours. We didn't even mind the process of moving.

Even with the joys of having a place of our own, we were all upset at the departure from Granny. "Don't think a thing of it," she said. "I may be an old woman, but I get around pretty good. I'll come to see you and you can come see me. You can't take Linda away from me." As we kissed her goodby, she said, "I love you, Zack. You've been like a son."

She hugged me. "I love you too, B.J. You're like one of my own."

She picked Linda up, "I'll always love you, darling. You're somebody special to me and always will be."

We went into a new phase of our lives, but Granny will never be forgotten. She did visit us and we still go to see her.

Chapter 19

All Grown Up

All was well with the world. Zack was teaching in college. We lived in our first house and we had Linda. She had both of us by the heart strings. We had very little money, but with all our other blessings, we didn't expect much. I had married a teacher, and I knew that our prospects of wealth ran from slim to none.

For recreation we took walks. Linda's legs were short, but her curiosity was enormous. It was August, and our late afternoon stroll had taken us to the other end of the block where curbs had been put in but no houses built yet. Linda sat on the curb. Her blonde curls shone in the evening light. There was a frown on her face. "What's this, Daddy?" she asked, holding out her small hand with the brown kernel inside.

"That's an acorn," Zack said.

I sat on the curb beside her. "When I was a little girl, like you. I used to pretend that acorns were teacups. The caps were the saucers and the nuts were the cups."

"If they're nuts, Daddy, can I eat them?"

Zack chuckled. "Back in the War Between The States people made coffee out of them, but it wasn't very good."

"Then why did they do that?"

"Because they didn't have anything else."

"Those poor people," she said.

106

In addition to being Zack's wife and Linda's mother, I was again a student. I went to classes and wrote my term papers with dedication and determination. I was going to get my degree.

Zack sat next to the aisle. Mamma, by now broad hipped and graying at the temples, sat next to him. Being a college professor had made Zack respectable in her eyes.

Linda, in her pink checked, lace trimmed, hopped-skirt dress, stood on the seat. To this day she has not forgiven me for making her wear socks with lace trim and white gloves. That day she stood very proud.

Beside her was my father. His snow white hair shone as he leaned on the cane he had made. "Albert can make anything," my grandmother said. He had made coat racks from cedar trees and book shelves that I still have.

I must have adjusted that mortar board a dozen times.

On the way to the graduation, Zack and I stopped at the drugstore for a final cup of coffee. We were sitting at the counter. My hands were shaking so that I held the cup with both hands. "I wish they had just mailed my degree," I said.

"Don't be silly," Zack said. "You'll be fine."

I was not fine. What if they discovered, at the last minute, that something was wrong and I wouldn't get my degree? Maybe I had not done something I should have. Wouldn't I look ridiculous in a cap and gown if I didn't graduate?

The dean touched me on the shoulder. I jumped. "Congratulations, B.J."

"Why, thank you," I smiled.

"It's been a pleasure working with you. I like good students," he said. He was one of my philosophy professors, and I was very fond of him. He encouraged you to think.

"By the way," he said, "When you go to graduate school, I'll be glad to give you a recommendation."

After he left, I turned to Zack. "Did you hear that? He didn't say 'if,' he said 'when.'"

"It's up to you."

"Wow, I'll have to think about that." I took a sip of my coffee. "It's just marvelous to have someone like that believe in you."

Zack covered my hand with his, "I believe in you, and so does Linda. That's all you need."

The music began and all of us stood in our places in line. I was grateful that I was not the first in line. The trick was to walk all the way down that aisle and across the stage without falling over my own feet.

"That's my mommy," Linda said out loud as I passed by.

"Do tell," someone nearby said.

I held my head high. I placed my feet sure-footed on the carpet. I had Zack and my beautiful Linda, and I was getting my degree. Outside, the birds were singing and somewhere in the distance a power mower was cutting grass.

The college president handed me my diploma with one hand and shook my other. "Congratulations," he said.

It was now certified that I had completed my college courses. I know it happened because I have pictures. There is one of Zack and me in our robes. There is also one of Zack, Linda and me in front of the building where I graduated. Linda has a gloved hand on each of our shoulders.

Education does not end with a degree, however. Perhaps that is where it begins. Each of my children has taught me a lot. First there was Linda and later Barbara and finally Skip. Friends, too, are a constant source of information. For example, my real estate freind whose death hit me like a sledgehammer.

"Why do we get along better with our friends than we sometimes do with relatives?" I asked her.

She smiled. "Because we choose our friends," she answered. "With relatives, it's pot luck."

You learn from what you see and what you hear, and, most of all, from what you feel. All your life you learn. You don't always like what you learn but you're in there trying.

This story ends with the awarding of my diploma. I stand before you in my cap and gown with my degree in my hand. My mind is filled with questions and my body with energy to face whatever the future has in store.

I have promised you a story and have told you several. I could write this book a dozen times and tell you other stories and not repeat one of these. A storyteller does not need to repeat. If you believe what I have written here, I have done my job well. If you don't, I have failed. Either way, I am a storyteller, a yarn spinner, a shanachie, and you can't believe a word I say.

Chapter 20

The Sting

There was a song, not too long ago, that said, "round, round, everything turn around. Round, round." It was not a new idea, except for those young enough to just be discovering it on their very own. The ancient Greeks knew, and we learn it as The Golden Mean. We call it fate, or God's Will, as it were, but, we all live by the basic rules of life whether we want to or not.

Mamma is gone now. She lived a long time. She drew her last breath with my hand on her brow.

What she left was mostly debris. I say "mostly" because she left some things of value. There is the silver watch that I found in the bottom of a sugar bowl, and Daddy's notebook, and several other things, but mostly, she left little things. There were plastic bags filled with bits of tissue, and Christmas cards at least twenty years old.

There were other things too. That is appropriate, since THINGS meant so much to her. People she treated like things, and in so doing, she outsmarted herself, because she left behind something that was grit in her craw. How could she be so careless? Did she know? Was this her way of getting under my skin from the grave?

Okay, old dear, you failed! You set me free.

"Hot dog," Zack said. "There has to be something here." He held up an envelope. "It says this envelope is not to be opened until both parents are dead."

They were. Daddy for a long time, and Mamma not long ago. Come to think of it, it was three weeks today.

I continued to stuff old church bulletins, and long ago paid bills in the plastic bag. How could anyone leave such a mess? She always did expect me to clean up after her.

"Holy shit," Zack said.

He got my attention.

"B.J., you were adopted."

I felt a chill go up my spine. All these years when I asked if I was adopted, I was told no, with a capital N and O.

"She swore us all to secrecy," Aunt Lydia said, when I called her. "I hope you won't love us any the less, because we have always loved you, and always will."

Of course I love Aunt Lydia. Now I know that the affection she has showered on me all these years was from the heart, and not because I was her sister's child. Her sister had no child.

I held that paper in my hand, and felt somehow lost. "Yesterday," I wrote my best friend, Hope, "I read Daddy's notebook, and it is like I never knew him. The young man who wanted so desperately to leave home, and the one who went off to war." I looked until I found one like him.

"That's okay " Zack said. "I think I'll keep you." He kissed my cheek.

After all of these years of trying to define who I am, I discover that I had no idea at all. How amazing! How ironic!

Well, old girl, if you thought you could destroy me with this tidbit, you were wrong. I do not crumble that easily. I had a mother somewhere who loved me enough to give me up. I salute you mother, wherever you are. You were indeed a noble lady.

You know, if I ever do get around to writing this book that I'm thinking about, I just might use my real name. I might sign it, for the very first time, "With fondest regards, Margaret Lee." I wonder if I'm related to the General.

The End